Interiors *in* Color

Interiors *in* Color

An Inspirational Guidebook for Color at Home

THUNDER BAY
P·R·E·S·S

Text and material on pages 11–296 appeared originally (in a slightly different form) in *Interiors in Red, Interiors in Yellow, Interiors in Blue,* and *Interiors in White,* copyright 1998, Rockport Publishers.

The text on pages 8–9 is reprinted with grateful acknowledgement to the author, Lesa Sawahata. This text appeared originally (in a slightly different form) in *The Color Harmony Workbook,* copyright 1999, Rockport Publishers.

First published in 2001 by
Thunder Bay Press
An imprint of the Advantage Publishers Group
5880 Oberlin Drive, San Diego, CA 92121-4794
www.advantagebooksonline.com

ISBN 1-57145-683-X
Library of Congress Cataloging-in-Publication Data available upon request.

Printed in China.

1 2 3 4 5 01 02 03 04 05

Cover Design: Leeann Leftwich
Cover Images: Lowrance Interiors, Inc. (top left), John Robert Wiltgen Design, photo by Jim Hedrich, Hedrich Blessing (bottom left), Carl Steele Associates (top right), Ruth Livingston Interior Design, photo by John Vaughan (bottom right)

❧ Contents ❧

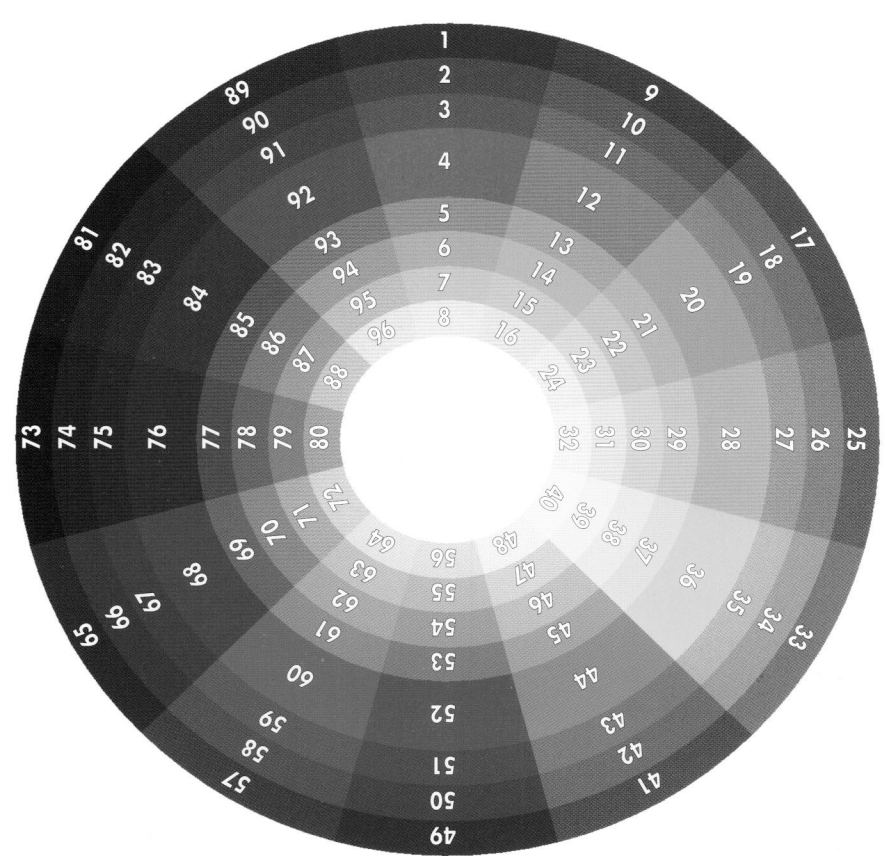

The beautiful interiors collected in these pages are offered to lend design inspiration to anyone seeking a precise command of color in all its delicious variety and moods.

We hope the many creative designs in these pages will arm you with ideas and creativity to solve any design project with the confidence of a pro.

To begin:

DEFINE the mood and goal of your project;

CHOOSE the color you feel best expresses this mood;

PLAY with the possibilities presented in the color schemes;

REFINE these color options down to the best possible color scheme.

Working with the Color Wheel

While it at first appears dazzling and complex, the color wheel is simplicity itself. Before discussing it, however, some basic color terminology is helpful.

A *hue* is simply a pure color—any color except white or black.

A *tint* is a hue mixed with white (red is a hue, pink is a tint).

A *shade* is a hue mixed with black (maroon is a shade of red).

A *tone* is a hue mixed with gray.

Chroma is the intensity or saturation of a hue—red has a higher chroma than pink or maroon.

Value describes the lightness and brightness of a color. Pink has a higher value than maroon; yellow, a higher value than blue.

The color wheel is composed of twelve basic hues: three primary, three secondary, and six tertiary. The colors in these families are equidistant on the color wheel.

Primary hues are red, blue, and yellow—colors that cannot be made by mixing other colors.

Secondary hues (green, orange, violet) are made by mixing two primary colors—red and yellow, for example, create orange.

Tertiary hues are made by mixing a primary with a secondary color—red-violet, yellow-orange, blue-green, blue-violet, yellow-green, and red-orange.

Complementary colors are opposites on the color wheel and, when mixed, will create a neutral.

Pure, high-chroma hues appear in the wide center band of the color wheel; look at numbers 4, 12, 20, 28, 36, 44, 52, 60, 68, 76, 84, and 92. Colors found in the four interior bands are tints, with various quantities of white added to the original hue; while the three outer bands are shades, with various amounts of black added to the original hue.

The Many Facets of Color

The emotional and psychological effects of color are undeniable, and it is in the facets of color—cold, hot, cool, warm, light, dark, pale, and bright—that the feeling produced by color has its strongest impact. On a cold day, we long for the leaping red flames of a fire; in the heat of summer, the mere sight of a shimmering blue-green pool is refreshing. We live in the constant play of color and feeling.

Cold Colors

To understand cold colors, think of ice, with its combined hues of blue, blue-green and green. These colors have the mind/body effect of slowing metabolism—someone in a "cold-colored" room will literally feel its cooling effects. Depending on its context, a fully-saturated blue can seem powerful, frigid, and austere; or it can be clean and fresh.

Hot Colors

Intense, fully-saturated red is like the essence of fire—a sense that applies to hot colors in general. Red has been proven to stimulate the physical body, increasing the level of activity as well as body temperature. Hot colors are attention-grabbing, making them a great choice for the focal points of a room.

Cool Colors

Cool colors are anchored in blue; unlike cold colors, however, they are blended with yellow and red, which creates a gorgeous range from green through blue through violet. These colors are perceived as soothing, calming, meditative, and peaceful, like a slowly-moving stream.

Warm Colors

Warm colors are based in red. Unlike hot colors, warm colors are softened with the addition of yellow, which creates a heady array of red-orange, orange, and yellow-orange. These direct, emotionally touching colors seem to reach out to us—an inviting, comforting aspect of warm colors that makes them natural for home interiors.

Light Colors

Light colors are barely colors at all—only the faintest hint of a hue is perceptible in these sheer, translucent colors. Because they are mostly white, light colors reflect the light around them, making a room—or a painting—seem to glow with a subtle illumination. Light colors open up space, making it feel larger and airier.

Dark Colors

Dark colors are strong, sober, and seem to diminish rather than expand space. They are often used as a means of contrasting lighter colors, and can convey a variety of moods—from dignity, tradition, and restraint to melancholy.

Pale Colors

Pale colors are tints—that is, hues combined with a large amount of white. Found in the central rings of the color wheel, these soft, tender pastels evoke a feeling of youth, innocence, gentleness, and romance.

Bright Colors

Bright colors are clear, distinctive, pure hues without a noticeable addition of white or black. These intense colors actually seem to vibrate; they are a keynote of the Pop Art movement of the 60s. Bright colors add dynamism and energy to interior design, even in small quantities.

Passion, heat, romance: the vibrancy of red is indisputable. A room saturated in red will be ablaze with color and demand attention. Even red accents will become the focal point of an otherwise neutral room. Red decorations will bring a touch of warmth and vitality to a room of cool colors. In combination with blue and yellow, red will add a sense of playfulness and energy. Red brings out the richness of color in a cherry table, and complements the rich tones of mahogany. The placement of color is as important as the choice of red itself: red in a living room will bring warmth and vitality, red in an entrance will be inviting, red in the dining room will add a regal atmosphere, and red in a bedroom will add drama and richness. Each person's emotional response to a color is entirely subjective. With all the spectrum to choose from, it is nearly impossible not to find the perfect red for any room of your home.

(right and below) INTERIOR DESIGN
Carl Steele Associates, Inc.

(opposite page) INTERIOR DESIGN
M. L. Slovack Design, Inc.

(above) Facilitated client's move from a large home to
a high-rise condominium by adapting client's furniture,
accessories and antiques to their new home.

INTERIOR DESIGN
Arlis Ede Interiors, Inc.

(below) Rich jewel tones and opulent furnishings, such as the silk velvet upholstery and the nineteenth-century Aubusson rug, dominate this contemporary version of the Imperial style.

INTERIOR DESIGN

Michael de Santis, Inc.

(right) Casual elegance dominates this mountain home situated on the side of a ski slope. Warm tones on the faux painted walls and rich cherry trim, floors and beams provide a dramatic backdrop for the country French furnishings and decorative accessories.

INTERIOR DESIGN

J. Powell & Associates, Inc.

(above) Against the backdrop of a rich red wall,
primitive masks crown this lofty study space and look
down upon furnishings from centuries after their time.

INTERIOR DESIGN

John Robert Wiltgen Design

Photo: Jim Hedrich, Hedrich Blessing

(above) The feeling of the ski
house is more European than
southwestern; the large Louis
XIV armoire makes a very
strong statement in the big
living room.

INTERIOR DESIGN
David Webster & Associates

(right) INTERIOR DESIGN
Kathleen Buoymaster, Inc.

Photo: Edward Gohlich

(left) A leather sofa, marble floor and vibrant painting highlight this beautifully appointed sitting area.

INTERIOR DESIGN
Kuckly Associates, Inc.

(left, below) A sunny, carefree room offers plenty of comfort, while serving as a showcase for a collection of pre-Columbian art.

INTERIOR DESIGN
Jennifer Garrigues, Inc.

(below) Refurbishment helped brighten and update St. Louis Mayor Freeman R. Bosley Jr.'s turn-of-the-century office in City Hall.

INTERIOR DESIGN
Carrie Brockman's Design Group

(above) In a room without architectural integrity,
simple early twentieth-century details, the clients'
collection of Cubist paintings, and neoclassical
furniture were combined to create a layered and
welcoming environment.

INTERIOR DESIGN
Brian J. McCarthy, Inc.

(left) Part of a master suite, this octagonal sitting room features a 20-foot turreted ceiling and French doors that open onto balconies overlooking a lake. French furnishings and sumptuous fabrics add to the aura of elegance.

INTERIOR DESIGN

Diane Wendell Interior Design

(above) New construction was given an old world feel by richly glazing walls, and using heavy textured fabrics in this den and library—private residence, Mr. and Mrs. Don Ware, Abbotsford, Nashville, Tennessee.

INTERIOR DESIGN

G. S. Hinsen Company

(right) Introducing a bold, modern fabric quickens the pulse of any room.

INTERIOR DESIGN
Bierly-Drake Associates

Photo: Sam Gray

(below) Family photos and mementos help personalize the quiet sitting room retreat off the master bedroom.

INTERIOR DESIGN
Meadowbank Designs, Inc.

(opposite page) Against a brilliant red wall, the poster becomes the room's focal point. Intense color draws the viewer's eye, and the black frame and white border intensify the effect.

INTERIOR DESIGN
Lovick Design

Photo: Art Grey

(above) Antiques, accessories, lighting, carpet, wallpaper, and reproduction settee—all with an "exotic" oriental feeling—create layers of pattern on pattern, complementing every surface in this sitting room.

INTERIOR DESIGN
Stingray Hornsby Interiors

(right) INTERIOR DESIGN
Dorothy H. Travis Interiors, Inc.

(right) A coffee table stained with rich Moroccan henna holds two rare Spanish colonial santos.

INTERIOR DESIGN
David Dalton Associates

(below) A cozy library features a bold mix of patterns and textures.

INTERIOR DESIGN
Diane Alpern Kovacs Interior Design, Inc.

(opposite page) Incorporating one or two strong design elements creates focus in rooms teeming with objects and collectibles. In the parlor, the most powerful elements are red walls and one large piece of art.

INTERIOR DESIGN
Claude Guidi

Photo: Steve Vierra

(below) Deep cherry walls with white moldings and a custom designed bookcase/dry bar made a bold statement softened by yellow florals, Persian rugs, and exquisite accessories. This room was designed to stand up to the test of time and eight grandchildren.

INTERIOR DESIGN
Lynn Robinson Interiors

(right) The entertainment center and tables designed by Bobbi Packer Designs are in the client's favorite colors. The space functions as the family's gathering room.

INTERIOR DESIGN
Bobbi Packer Designs

(*below*) The oversize living room of this residence has as its focus the magnificent formal gardens beyond the large bay window.

INTERIOR DESIGN

Trilogy

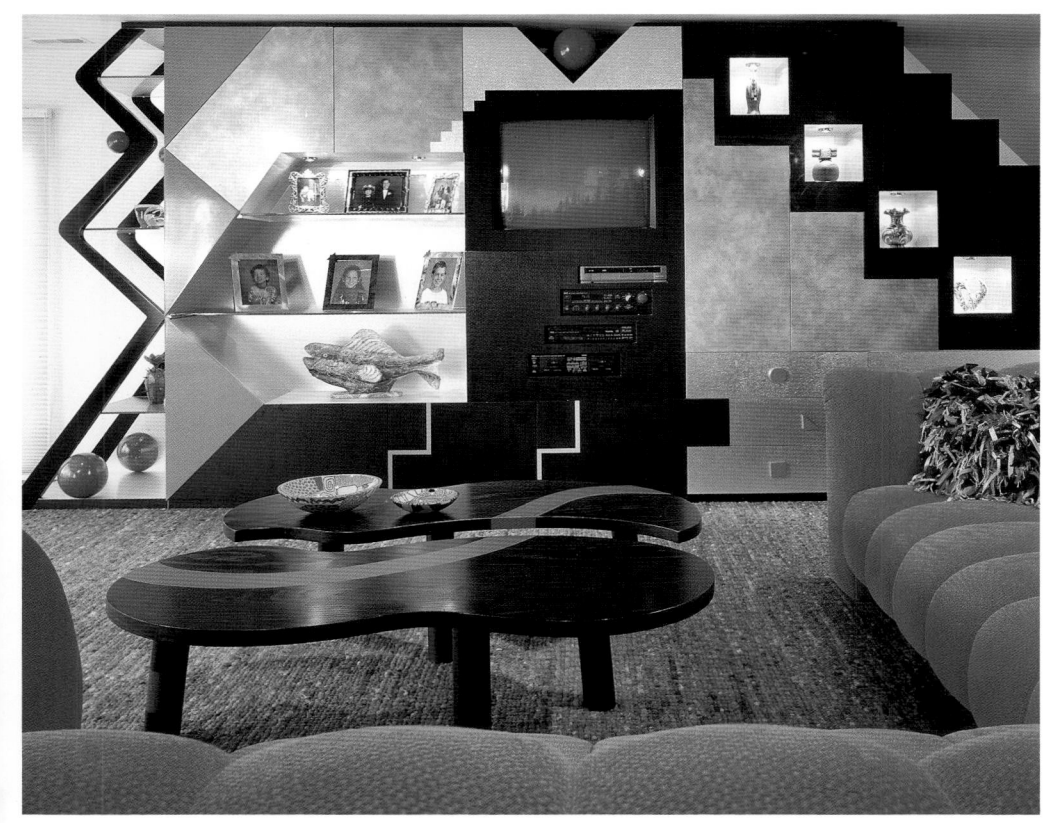

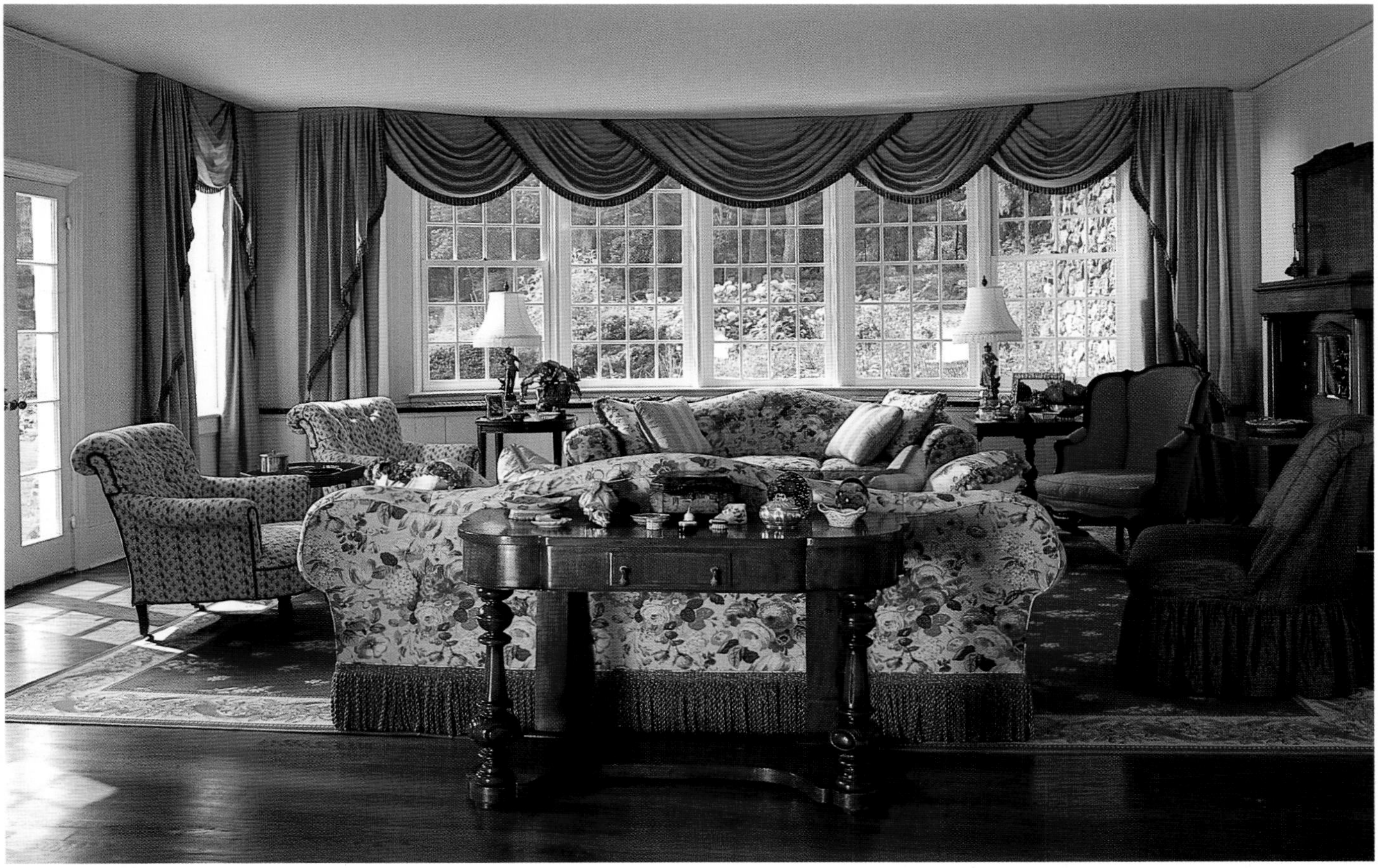

(above) INTERIOR DESIGN

Barbara Lazarus

(right) INTERIOR DESIGN

Clifford Stiles McAlpin Interiors, Inc.

(above) INTERIOR DESIGN

Claude Guidi

Photo: Steve Vierra

(above) INTERIOR DESIGN
Cricket Interiors

(above) The owner's love of animals
is reflected in a range of details,
from elephants parading across the
valance to the ceramic pieces that
grace tabletops and bookshelves.

INTERIOR DESIGN

Fran Murphy & Associates

The upholstered walls of the room add an extra warmth to this niche, which contains a drop arm sofa and a chinoise coffee table set with antique decanters and glasses.

INTERIOR DESIGN

Antine Associates

The warmth of the room is achieved by using a mixture of elegant fabrics, fine antiques and collectables, and wonderfully comfortable upholstery. The chinoise secretary is seventeenth century, the bull's eye mirror eighteenth century, and the rug later nineteenth century. The walls are upholstered in Scottish wool woven in a Russian pattern.

INTERIOR DESIGN

Antine Associates

(above) INTERIOR DESIGN

Judy McMurray

Photo: Steve Vierra

(above) Rich colored walls
and furnishings combined with
the strong natural light provide
a cozy haven for reading,
watching television, or enjoying
the company of friends and
relatives.

INTERIOR DESIGN
Sue Wenk Interior Design Inc.

(below) Warm, comfortable setting combines French and
English antiques with collections
of Meissen, Derby and Imari.

INTERIOR DESIGN
Rodgers Menzies Interior Design

(above) A crisp country English setting is created in this historic Pennsylvania farmhouse. Antiques subtly fill the room, and color and pattern mix like old friends.

INTERIOR DESIGN
Meadowbank Designs, Inc.

(right) INTERIOR DESIGN
Arlene Semel & Associates, Inc.

(below) To make this formal living room more approachable while still imparting an air of elegance, the warm tones of the Oushak rug are used throughout, while a collection of interesting and unusual accessories punctuates the seating areas.

INTERIOR DESIGN

C. Weaks Interiors, Inc.

(left) An intimate fireplace area combines wood and stone with warm, jewel-toned colorations in the antique area rug and occasional seating.

INTERIOR DESIGN

Ron Hefler

(below) Room With a View— all upholstery custom designed and built, eclectic mixture of antiques and styles

INTERIOR DESIGN

Chambers Interiors and Associates, Inc.

(left) This library, formerly a garage, serves as the informal gathering place for a large family.

INTERIOR DESIGN
Trilogy

(above) A sofa from Baker Furniture and an antique Irish Chippendale tea table are just two of the highlights in this living room. The painting above the mantel—"Going Home"—is 150 years old.

INTERIOR DESIGN
Myrl Talkington Designs

(above) Rich colors, exquisite furnishings and an abundance of architectural details work together to create the ultimate in refined living. Note the tromp l'oeil "alcoves" on the right.

INTERIOR DESIGN

Gerhard Design Group

(left) An intricately orchestrated palette and elaborate detailing conspired with English, French and Italian antiques to create a rich eclectic interior of distinct personality.

INTERIOR DESIGN

Eberlein Design Consultants Ltd.

(below) Custom designed floral rug offers foundation for fresh, vibrant color scheme; warms a large room overlooking pool and lake.

INTERIOR DESIGN

Rodgers Menzies Interior Design

(right) Capitalizing on an already dark room, the deep green walls create a serene setting for a smallish living room and present the perfect back-drop for "Hairdresser," a 1948 painting by Russian-born Simka Simkhovitch.

(below right) "Cochise" the howling coyote sets the tone for this whimsy filled proch, a favorite summer-time retreat.

INTERIOR DESIGN

Busch and Associates

54

(above) INTERIOR DESIGN

Kuhl Design Associates, Inc.

(above) INTERIOR DESIGN

Cricket Interiors

(above) A country library in an American pre-
Revolutionary house has been created in an eclectic
manner. A traditional linen floral fabric and needlepoint
rug have been combined with a mirrored wall and
Chinese lacquered coffee table.

INTERIOR DESIGN
Scott Salvator, Inc.

(above) Antique French furnishings collected by the owners grace this new town house.

INTERIOR DESIGN
Clifford Stiles McAlpin Interiors, Inc.

(right) INTERIOR DESIGN
M.L. Slovack Design, Inc.

(above) A Gothic revival sitting room is born by
vaulting a previously flat ceiling and ading cabinetry and moldings.

INTERIOR DESIGN
Henry Johnstone & Co.

(above) A heightened sense of
formality is accomplished with
heavily festooned windows,
damask wallcovering, silk upholstery and elegant accessories.

INTERIOR DESIGN
John Henry Sherman, Jr. Interiors

(right) INTERIOR DESIGN
Akins and Aylesworth

(right) INTERIOR DESIGN

Susan Kroeger, Ltd.

(below) INTERIOR DESIGN

J. Westerfield Antiques & Interiors, Inc.

(above) Dramatic use of colorful fluid
forms makes this "L"-shaped family
room an exciting place to expand
one's horizons.

INTERIOR DESIGN
Pedlar's Village Interior Design

(above) An Old World map on faux parchment was commissioned for the ceiling of this library. The furniture, artwork, antique Persian rug and leather wall panels create a rich, worldly effect.

INTERIOR DESIGN
Suzanne Stacey McCallen / G. S. Hinsen Compoany

(above) A bronze "Big Bird" and an intriguing sculpture on the coffee table are among the many special collectibles that give this apartment a flavor all its own.

INTERIOR DESIGN

S & B Interiors, Inc.

(lef) INTERIOR DESIGN

Kuhl Design Associates, Inc.

(right) INTERIOR DESIGN
Joan Halperin/Interior Design

(below) Many cherished possessions fit comfortably into this vibrantly colorful keeping room.

INTERIOR DESIGN
Rodgers Menzies Interior Design

(above) A crisp country English setting
is created in this historic Pennsylvania
farmhouse. Antiques subtly fill the
room, and color and pattern mix
like old friends.

INTERIOR DESIGN
Meadowbank Designs, Inc.

(right) INTERIOR DESIGN
Ellen Sosnow Interiors

(below) INTERIOR DESIGN
Browns Interiors, Inc.

(above) INTERIOR DESIGN

Joan Spiro Interiors

(right) Turnberry Isle Beauty Salon

INTERIOR DESIGN

JoyCe Stolberg Interiors, Inc.

(right) Louis, Boston

INTERIOR DESIGN

Stedila Design, Inc.

(right) The dining room in this historical house, built circa 1750 and later relocated to an oceanfront site, possesses a wonderful Normandy feel. An oil portrait of Mrs. Baker —the original owner of the house—presides over the long room at last, after residing in the attic for some time. The color scheme is now brighter, bridging the past to the present.

INTERIOR DESIGN
Alexis E. Benne Interiors

(below right) A mix of antiue chairs with Fortuny upholstery and modern architecture creates a contemporary and romantic setting in this restaurant.

INTERIOR DESIGN
L.B.D.A. Design Associates, Inc.

(opposite page) Modern art, new furniture, and the unexpected red color of the mantel add personal flair to a house with traditional architecture.

INTERIOR DESIGN
Ida Goldstein

Photo: Steve Vierra

(above) The elements used in this small, square dining room were selected to make maximum use of space while highlighting the sense of intimacy. Replacing the traditional rectangular table and long sideboard with a round table and pair of demilune cabinets allows for ease of movement without sacrificing seating or storage.

INTERIOR DESIGN

C. Weaks Interiors, Inc.

(right) INTERIOR DESIGN

J. Dayvault & Associates

(below right) Here, sleek design is accented with a Southwestern flair. The older cabinets feature an autumn red heirloom finish. Reflections of light bounce from the absolute black granite tile countertops. Eagle, Colorado.

INTERIOR DESIGN

Thurston Kitchen & Bath

(below) This eclectic living room works
in large part because of its unifying
color scheme of red, brown, gold,
and soft yellow.

INTERIOR DESIGN
Samuel Botero Associates

Photo: Phillip H. Ennis

(right) Permanent murals set the color palette,
individual dining tables counterbalance formality.

INTERIOR DESIGN
Howard Snoweiss Design Group

PHOTO
Steven Brooke

(left) Antique Irish Chippendale chairs, a Serapi rug, and a period mahogany sheraton server work together to create a breathtaking effect.

INTERIOR DESIGN
Myrl Talkington Designs

(below) Hand-painted glazed walls, silk lined damask draped windows and a 19th century French chandelier set the stage for entertaining meals.

INTERIOR DESIGN
Julie Lanterman Interior Designs

~ Yellow Interiors ~

The neutrality of yellow sometimes belies its importance in the color scheme of a room. Pale yellows will add warmth to a room otherwise stark in its whiteness, yet yellow is neutral enough to showcase the more daring colors in the room. Though yellow can recede into the background, it just as easily can become the focal point: Think of a bright yellow sunburst on a dark background. From pale, sandy yellow to bright tulip yellow to glittery gold, the opportunities and choices for using the color yellow in a room's color palette are infinite. Sunshine yellow brings happiness to a room. Pair yellow with purple for a royal effect. Primary yellow energizes when combined with red and blue. Sometimes yellow in a room is not from purposeful color choices, rather, our incandescent lighting has yellow undertones, giving a glowing, warm cast to a room. This warm, cozy atmosphere can be further enhanced with yellow walls and accessories. Yellow, in any shade or tone, is perfect for every room of the house. Mix and match it: the opportunities are yours!

(above) Designed for a man with eclectic tastes, a
non-traditional color scheme complements the mix
of traditional and modern furniture in this study/
bedroom.

INTERIOR DESIGN
Interior Options

(right) INTERIOR DESIGN
Sheila Britz Design, Inc.

(above) This superb living room hosts an
exuberant meeting of classical, rococo, and
contemporary styles. Note how the fabrics
and upholstery alternate between the past
and present.

INTERIOR DESIGN

Barry Dixon

Photo: Gordon Beall

(above) A lively floral pattern makes a splash in this vibrant family room. The walls and furniture create an intimate atmosphere emphasizing relaxed formality—a reflection of the client's lifestyle and personality.

(left) Combined with detailed architectural paneling, the floral wallcovering appears to be clinging from a garden trellis.

INTERIOR DESIGN

V-3 Design

(above) Combine pastels with intense, dark color to create a room of lively contrasts. Here, the butter-colored walls and pastel upholstery are the perfect foil for the highly colored and patterned rug and dark wood finishings.

INTERIOR DESIGN
Richard Fitzgerald

Photo: Steve Vierra

(above) INTERIOR DESIGN

Barry Dixon

Photo: Gordon Beall

(above) A very small living room in a carriage house presented the challenge of making use of existing furniture. A periwinkle blue ceiling and linen-colored walls create a palette that easily blends with all colors.

INTERIOR DESIGN
Elizabeth Read Weber, ASID

(left) INTERIOR DESIGN
Jane Crary Interior Design

(above) A bejeweled daffodil-yellow
and red room enhances a superb art
and antique collection, making for a
dramatic room day and night..

INTERIOR DESIGN
James R. Irving, ASID

(above) INTERIOR DESIGN

Barbara Lazarus

(above) All furniture by Letelier & Rock is custom-made for this room. Linen scrims at the windows are also by Letelier & Rock. The room features ash-wood and steel lamps, brushed steel sconces, ashwood sofas with zip-off cushions, and bookcases.

INTERIOR DESIGN
Letelier & Rock Design, Inc.

(right) Classical elements play beautifully in this living and dining room in shades of warm white—private residence, Constance Woolsey, Nashville, Tennessee.

INTERIOR DESIGN
G. S. Hinsen Company

(above) INTERIOR DESIGN

James R. Irving, ASID

(above) Like the sun in the sky, blue and yellow
are a natural combination. Here, prints, patterns,
and objects from around the world draw attention
in an intimate space of warm and cool, sunny
and subdued colors.

INTERIOR DESIGN

Ann Sullivan

Photo: Steve Vierra

(below) Mauve pink walls and a lovely English floral fabric, Carlotta, offset a superb collection of rare and important antiques and give a sense of serenity.

INTERIOR DESIGN
James R. Irving, ASID

(above) INTERIOR DESIGN

Tomar Lampert Associates

Photo: Chuck White

(above) New construction was given
an old world feel by richly glazing
walls, and using heavy textured fabrics
in this den and library—private residence, Mr. and Mrs. Don Ware,
Abbotsford, Nashville, Tennessee.

INTERIOR DESIGN
G. S. Hinsen Company

(right) Cheerful furnishings create an
aura of casual elegance without detract-
ing from the room's striking architecture.

INTERIOR DESIGN
Diane Wendell Interior Design

(above) The rich color tapestry on the walls coordinates with the elegant antique Oriental rug to give this room texture. Deep, plush window treatments enhance the relaxed, but traditional, interior.

INTERIOR DESIGN
Akins and Aylesworth, Ltd.

(above) Glazed pale lemon makes this San Francisco living room sunny even on the foggiest days. A smattering of Oriental floral chintz from Clarence House adds to the colors in the impressionist and contemporary paintings. The dhurrie carpet helps maintain a contemporary point of view, but the furnishings are a mix of traditional and modern styles.

INTERIOR DESIGN
Mario Buatta Incorporated

(above) INTERIOR DESIGN

Antine Associates Interior Design

(above) An adult, city apartment has soaring views of
Central Park. The pale colors and selected antiques
give a soft and stable background to daily life with
treetop views. Originally a two-story artist's studio, the
balcony now serves as the master bedroom.

INTERIOR DESIGN

David Ripp Incorporated

INTERIOR DESIGN

Clifford Stiles McAlpin Interiors, Inc.

(right) INTERIOR DESIGN

Oetgen Design and Fine Antiques, Inc.

(above) The warmth of the room is achieved by using
a mixture of elegant fabrics, fine antiques and collectibles, and wonderfully comfortable upholstery. The
chinoise secretary is seventeenth century, the bull's eye
mirror eighteenth century, and the rug late nineteenth
century. The walls are upholstered in Scottish wool
woven in a Russian pattern.

INTERIOR DESIGN

Antine Associates

INTERIOR DESIGN

Clifford Stiles McAlpin Interiors, Inc.

(above) INTERIOR DESIGN
Coulson-Hamlin

(right) The parlour of historic Sweetbrush Estate, Austin, Texas (1852) in its happiest palette of its 140 years. Lead print fabric—Brunschwig-Fils.

INTERIOR DESIGN
Nicholson Interiors

(above) INTERIOR DESIGN

Jane Crary Interior Design

(above) Reading or relaxing by the fire on a
"tete-a-tete" designed by Antine—formality
with a huge accent on comfort.

INTERIOR DESIGN

Antine Associates

(above) Sophisticated with its
mix of formal and country antique
pieces, this charming weekend retreat
incorporates cheerful fabrics and
persian rugs.

INTERIOR DESIGN

Ellen Korney Associates

(left) INTERIOR DESIGN

Ricki Tucker Interiors and Cabin Antiques

(above) This end of a formal living room opens onto a covered loggia, allowing an unusual blending of indoor and out-door furnishings, including a fire screen fashioned from a garden gate. Mirrored surfaces add light and space.

INTERIOR DESIGN
Barry Dixon, Inc.

(left) Elegance is carefully balanced with the help of a French screen, Italian console and chintz slipcovered chairs.

INTERIOR DESIGN
Rodgers Menzies Interior Design

(below) INTERIOR DESIGN
Creative Decorating

Photo: David Livingston

(above) INTERIOR DESIGN

Anne Weinberg Designs, Inc.

(above) INTERIOR DESIGN

Robert Pope Associates, Inc.

(above) The sleeping porch of
"Leighton," *The Fred Rand House.*

INTERIOR DESIGN

Sanford R. Thigpen Interiors, Inc.

(below) INTERIOR DESIGN

Kathy Harman/The Corner Cupboard Antiques and Interiors

(above) Designing beautiful interiors requires magnificent sources, attention to detail and the ability to capture the essence of the client's dreams, as shown in this elegant traditional interior. The feature of the room is the antique eighteenth century Aubusson rug. Antique furnishings and accessories were collected from France and England and are blended with luxurious fabrics, upholstery and contemporary art.

INTERIOR DESIGN
Ann Platz & Co.

(right) Timeless elegance fills the living room of this 6,000 square foot New York apartment that had been gutted prior to renovation.

INTERIOR DESIGN
V-3 Design

(above) Walls, ceilings, moldings and columns
form a background against which the best of
the old is combined with the best of the new.

INTERIOR DESIGN

V-3 Design

(left and below) INTERIOR DESIGN
Ricki Tucker Interiors and Cabin Antiques

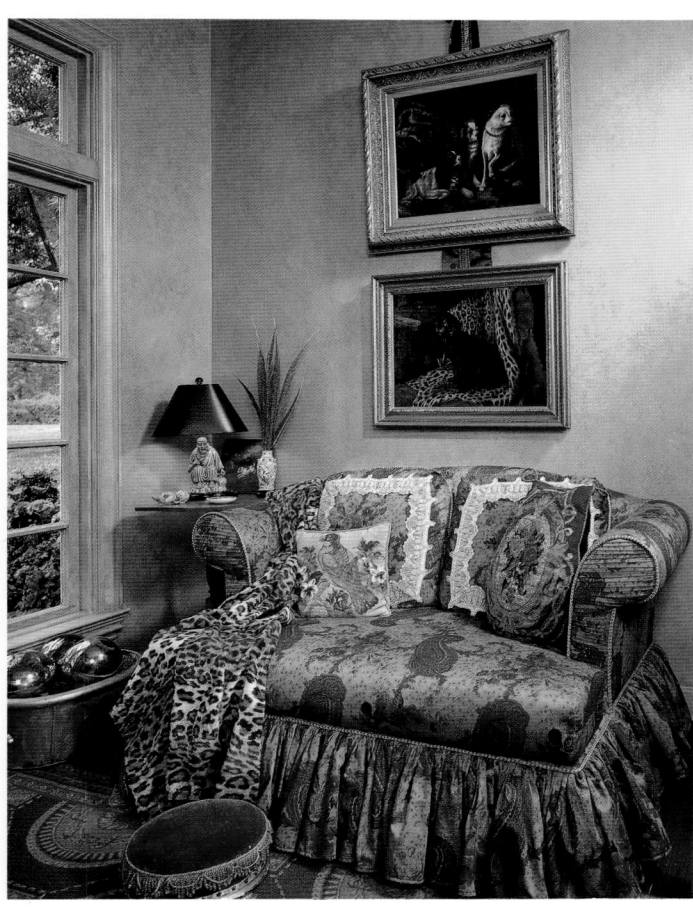

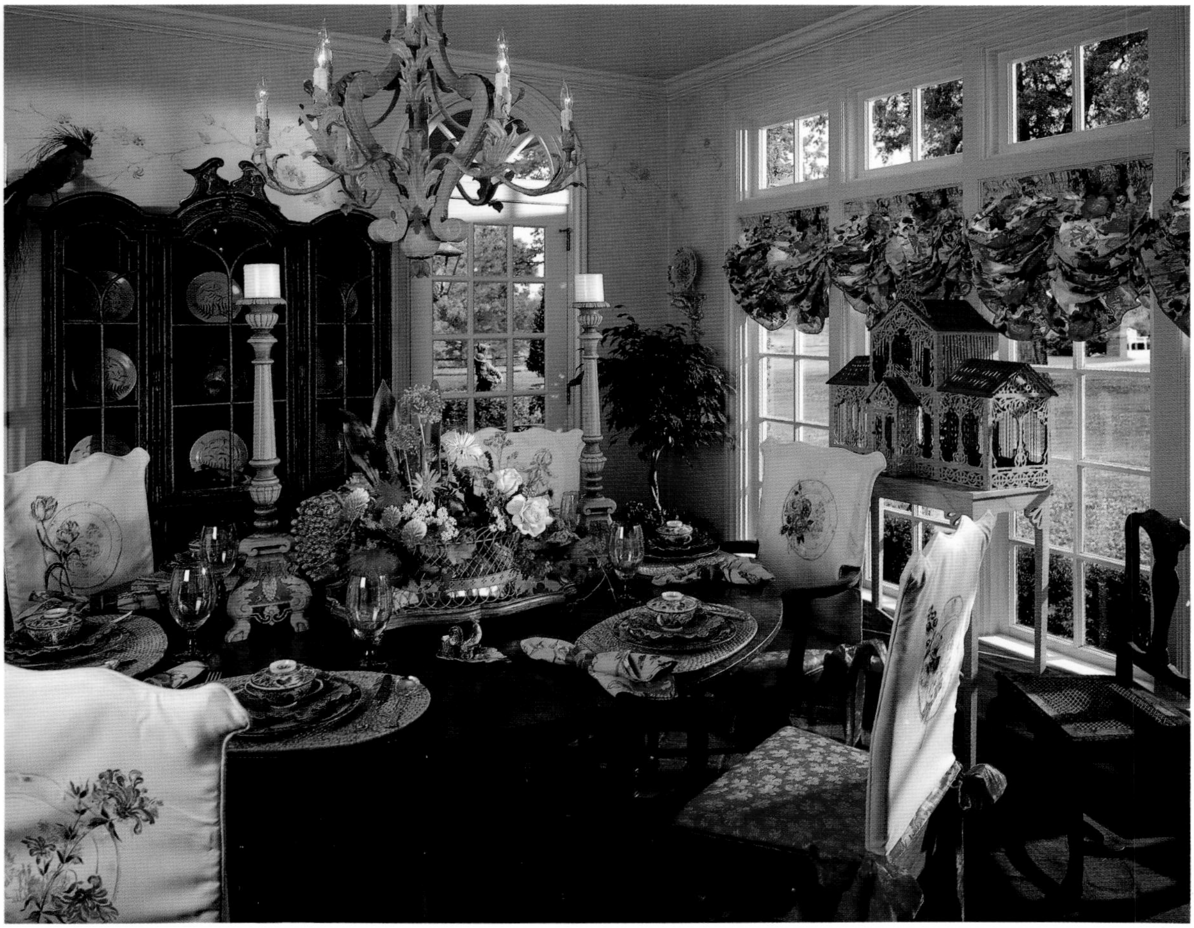

(below) A golden master suite, spare yet elegant, serves as an inviting private retreat in this Palm Beach, Florida, home.

INTERIOR DESIGN

Stedila Design, Inc.

(above) INTERIOR DESIGN

Anne Weinberg Designs, Inc.

(below) INTERIOR DESIGN

James R. Irving, ASID

(right) The living room of a Greek Revival
cottage in Florida reflects the owner's love
of color and design.

INTERIOR DESIGN

Clifford Stiles McAlpin Interiors, Inc.

(above) The grand living room of a Hudson River property projects designer Barbara Ostrom's ability to recreate period architecture, cabinetry, columns and ·moldings while orchestrating color and texture, fabrics and furnishings, in a large scale setting.

INTERIOR DESIGN

Barbara Ostrom Associates, Inc.

(left) This Palm Beach living room encompasses the various styles of the client's collections.

INTERIOR DESIGN

Barbara Lazarus

(right) Black highlights in the fabrics and seating contrast with a serene sea-green background. The Clarence House print contains all the colors that appear throughout the home. Note the combination of comfortable upholstery and antique case pieces. Antique majolica is displayed in the wall cabinet.

(below) Strong color creates an inviting family room. The checkered upholstery echoes the geometry of the square panels in the ceiling and windows.

INTERIOR DESIGN

Barbara Metzler Interior Design, Inc.

(right) INTERIOR DESIGN

Muriel Hebert, Inc.

(above) The herringbone wood floor and antique
rug highlight a medley of patterns and textures.

INTERIOR DESIGN

Deutsch/Parker Design Ltd.

(above) Antiques accent a space that
exudes a cutting-edge attitude.

INTERIOR DESIGN

Freya Serabian

Photo: Steve Vierra

(left) INTERIOR DESIGN

Barbara Lazarus

(left) The Kips Bay Showhouse in New York boasts
an atelier bridge of steel and aluminum grille,
accessed by hidden stairs behind the cracked-plaster wall. Indicative of the Stedila Design style is the
mixture of classic furnishings with contemporary
materials and architectural details.

INTERIOR DESIGN

Stedila Design, Inc.

(above) French furnishings and architectural details add grandeur to a spacious sitting area. Note the custom cord and tassels on the French empire sofa.

INTERIOR DESIGN

Edward C. Turrentine Interior Design Inc.

(above) Along the side of a formal room, a canted mirror casually reflects as much light and space as the flanking windows. A custom plaster ceiling is painted like the wall and trim for unity and height.

INTERIOR DESIGN

Barry Dixon, Inc.

(above) Inspiring design elements
breathe character into a functional
space that's conducive to creativity
and reflection.

INTERIOR DESIGN
Judith Lynne Interior Design

(right) INTERIOR DESIGN
Ellen Sosnow Interiors

(above) This living room evolved after a renovation of a newly empty nest household. The client wanted a comfortable room with abundant seating capacity. Bookcases were added for symmetry and to showcase the client's collectibles, art, and family photographs. Bright colors were used throughout.

INTERIOR DESIGN

Rita St. Clair Associates, Inc.

(above) Bright, comfortable and inviting, this living room makes dramatic use of textures, colors and furniture styles.

(left) Elegant antique furnishings greet guests with a traditional welcome in this foyer.

INTERIOR DESIGN

Sirola Designs, Ltd.

(above) INTERIOR DESIGN

James R. Irving, ASID

(left) New construction is given the feeling of
a 200-year-old manor house with the addition
of a stone wall and beautifully oiled dark walnut
floors. The French Bressane armoire in walnut
burl and cherry, circa 1820, and beautiful
Aubusson rug further this look of an age rich
with tradition.

INTERIOR DESIGN

Meadowbank Designs, Inc.

(above) Lemon walls with off-white moldings frame a
collection of porcelain floral plates and paintings. The
simple dotted Swiss fabric works well with the pink
plaid curtain and bed ensemble. The rose-patterned
carpet sits on green-and-white bow carpeting (both
from Stark). The oval mirror is English. The upholstery is
designed by Mario Buatta for John Widdicomb
Company and covered in fabrics from Brunschwig and
Fils.

INTERIOR DESIGN
Mario Buatta Incorporated

(above) INTERIOR DESIGN

Lowrance Interiors, Inc.

(left) A rich balance of warm colors, textures, fabrics and furnishings combines to give this jewelry store an ambiance of gracious luxury.

INTERIOR DESIGN

SPACES/Interior Design

Photo: John C. Lindy

(left) The owner's multitude of collections and love of color are expressed.

(below left) A porch is now correspondence, game and bar multifunctions.

INTERIOR DESIGN
Klingmans of Grand Rapids

(right) Crisp marble floors and glass blocks create a dramatic backdrop for a formal contemporary dining area.

INTERIOR DESIGN
Tomar Lampert Associates

(above) The owners of this pied-a-terre have an extensive contemporary art collection, including a three-dimensional painting by Arman, and bronze sculpture by Anthony Caro.

INTERIOR DESIGN

Carl Steele Associates, Inc.

(left) Combined with detailed architectural paneling, the floral wallcovering appears to be clinging from a garden trellis.

INTERIOR DESIGN

V-3 Design

Blue: the color of the ocean, the color of the sky. From faded blue jeans to sapphires, blue is all around us. Each different shade of blue will draw a different emotional response from you. Pale blues will add a sense of tranquillity, a peace not found in the starkness of plain white. Bright blues will energize a room, especially in combination with the other primary colors, red and yellow. Blues and greens mixed in different shades and variations will recall a sunny tropical ocean or the pale serenity of a summer meadow. Blue lends itself to patterns, from the popular gingham to delft china. The color alone will not create the total effect. Shiny blue surfaces will reflect the light and create a different effect than a matte or textured surface. Consider the natural and unnatural light sources that will surround blue in a living room, or the shaded light that appears in a bedroom. Light and texture factor into the final appearance of the color. From accent pillows to furniture to walls to curtains, in flat washes or intricate patterns, blue can be the perfect choice of color for every room of the home. The choice depends on you.

(above) A 1970s house with dark pine post-and-beam construction, rough cedar, and moss rock was renovated into an airy contemporary residence highlighting expansive views of the mountains in Snowmass, Colorado. Evening sunsets cast blue and purple hues, inspiring the use of rich jewel tones against a light background.

(right) Original 4x4 posts were sheathed in drywall to form large columns and connected with a glass wall in the dining room to enhance privacy. The contemporary Navajo weaving above the fireplace adds to the regional uniqueness of the space.

INTERIOR DESIGN

Sara Zook Designs, Ltd.

(opposite page) INTERIOR DESIGN

Riemenschneider Design Associates, Inc.

(right) Cool blue fabric offers a soothing corner for reading and relaxation.

INTERIOR DESIGN

Judith Lynne Interior Design

(below) An eclectic room, warm and inviting. The built-in units conceal a large screen television and a multitude of storage.

INTERIOR DESIGN

Peter Charles Interiors

(above and left) Mirrors enlarge the living and dining areas which have an art deco influence alive with color and exotic traditional accents.

INTERIOR DESIGN
Rhonda A. Roman Interiors
Detriot, Michigan

(above) Elements of the British "Raj" in India accentuate this sun-filled garden room. A settee and chair of carved, painted teak provide seating around a faux leopard-skin floorcloth; a screen depicting European neo-classic architecture forms a back-drop amid a variety of plants.

INTERIOR DESIGN
Horne International Designs, Inc.

(left) INTERIOR DESIGN
Blair Design Associates, Inc.

(above) An eclectic mix of silks, velvets, linens, and taffetas enhances unusual furnishings and accessories throughout the salon. A theatrical Andrew Dubreuil iron and glass torchiere is set against a backdrop of a mirror and satin and taffeta curtains.

INTERIOR DESIGN
Dennis Rolland, Inc.

(right) Motoakasaka House, Fukuoka, Japan

INTERIOR DESIGN
Ronald Bricke & Associates, Inc.

(left and below) INTERIOR DESIGN
Jane J. Marsden Antiques & Interiors, Inc.

(left) INTERIOR DESIGN
Mary W. Delany Interior Design

(below) This scheme is essentially monochromatic, but is stimulating to the eye because of the rich combination of dark blue, bright blue, and subtle gray. The solid colors give the sculptural lines of the contemporary furniture crisp definition.

INTERIOR DESIGN
Bedroom by Cassina

(opposite page) An artistic design element sets the stage for an expansive living area.

INTERIOR DESIGN
Susan Fredman & Associates, Ltd.

(right) One of Addison Mizner's 1922 oceanfront mansions, this Palm Beach, Florida, residence features an addition that's historically accurate but furnished for today's lifestyle.

INTERIOR DESIGN
Stedila Design, Inc.

(below) A classic modern house, built in 1960, restored to its original splendor with a new liveability. The rug is an original design by Annie Albers, artist and wife of Josef Albers, the famous color theorist.

INTERIOR DESIGN
David Ripp Incorporated

(above) A dining room in a
Federal house features antique
furniture, drawings by Robert
Motherwell, and custom carpeting by Stark.

INTERIOR DESIGN
Carl Steele Associates, Inc.

(above) A blue antique robe and exquisite Chinese procelains punctuate an otherwise neutral living room.

INTERIOR DESIGN
Ginny Stine Interiors, Inc.

(right) An Eastern sitting room shows influence of Moroccan and Turkish ornaments and architecture.

INTERIOR DESIGN
Horne International Designs, Inc.

(opposite page) INTERIOR DESIGN
Carl Steele Associates, Inc.

(above) Strong architectural details in the fireplace and windows set the mood for this comfortable living room. Tiered gardens of flowers reflect the soft palette inside, while walnut floors underscore the soft warmth of the pastel Oriental rugs and Chinese porcelains.

INTERIOR DESIGN
Sara Zook Designs, Ltd.

(right) The lacquered screen and Chinese flower pots incorporate more subtle versions of the vivid color palette of this space.

INTERIOR DESIGN
Robert E. Tartarini Interiors

Photo: Dennis Krukowski

(below) Vibrant cool blue walls pronounce the red
antique painted furniture and add depth to the room.
Crisp blue and white fabrics from Cowtan & Tout
and accents of red maintain the integrity of the
atmosphere.

INTERIOR DESIGN

Elizabeth Read Weber, ASID, LLC

(above) The metal and wood blend
of the tables, contemporary lines of
the furniture, and narrow shelf along
the wall displaying old treasures,
such as a scale and wooden boxes,
work well together.

INTERIOR DESIGN
Mark Zeff

Photo: Mario Ruiz

(above) In the living room of this residence, a collection of framed images is given emphasis mounted on a blue-tinted glass mirror. Vintage bowling balls from the 1940s are treated like moveable pieces of art.

(left) In the dining room, a collection of Robert Mapplethorpe photographs are juxtaposed with a pop-art cabinet with custom-designed buffet wings. The colors of the cabinet and buffet are picked up in the horizontal stripes of the crown molding, which is painted to resemble the coat of a Dalmatian.

INTERIOR DESIGN
Al Evans Interiors
Photos: Dan Forer

(above) The offices of an investment firm
provide residential elegance and comfort
without sacrificing efficiency and durability.

INTERIOR DESIGN
Solis-Betancourt

(right) Note how the palm tree and blue
door frames add splashes of color to a
living space that relies on simple, comfortable white furnishings.

INTERIOR DESIGN
C. M. Wright, Inc.

(below) Renovating a room not part of a historical house, the designer aimed for a contemporary nautical feeling more conductive to its summer residents. Previously dark, this room is now much lighter in feeling, with whisper white walls.

INTERIOR DESIGN
Alexis E. Benné Interiors

(top right) The owner of this Southampton, NY farmhouse wanted to display a collection of Russian furnishings and accessories in a formal environment. The yellow and blue color scheme goes from the palest shade of yellow to brilliant blue in a sophisticated take on a tried-and-true color combination.

(bottom right) This dramatic salon for a famous New York modern art dealer was designed to complement a vibrant collection of art. The room rates a variety of unique and luxurious finishes created by a talented group of artisans, including a graphite ceiling and pigmented beeswax encaustic walls. The daring jewel-tone color scheme was inspired by the Stephen Mueller painting over the sofa.

INTERIOR DESIGN
Dennis Rolland, Inc.

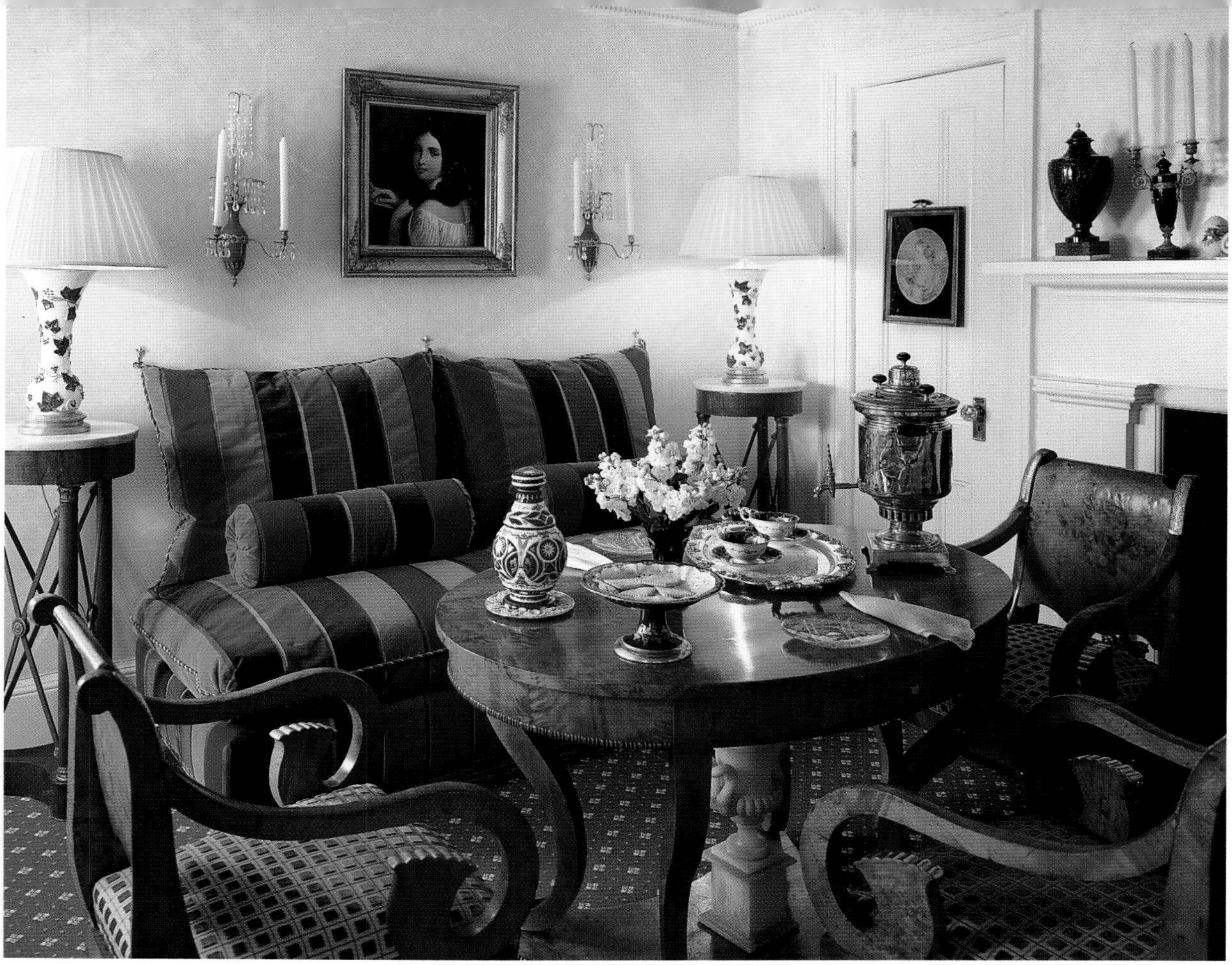

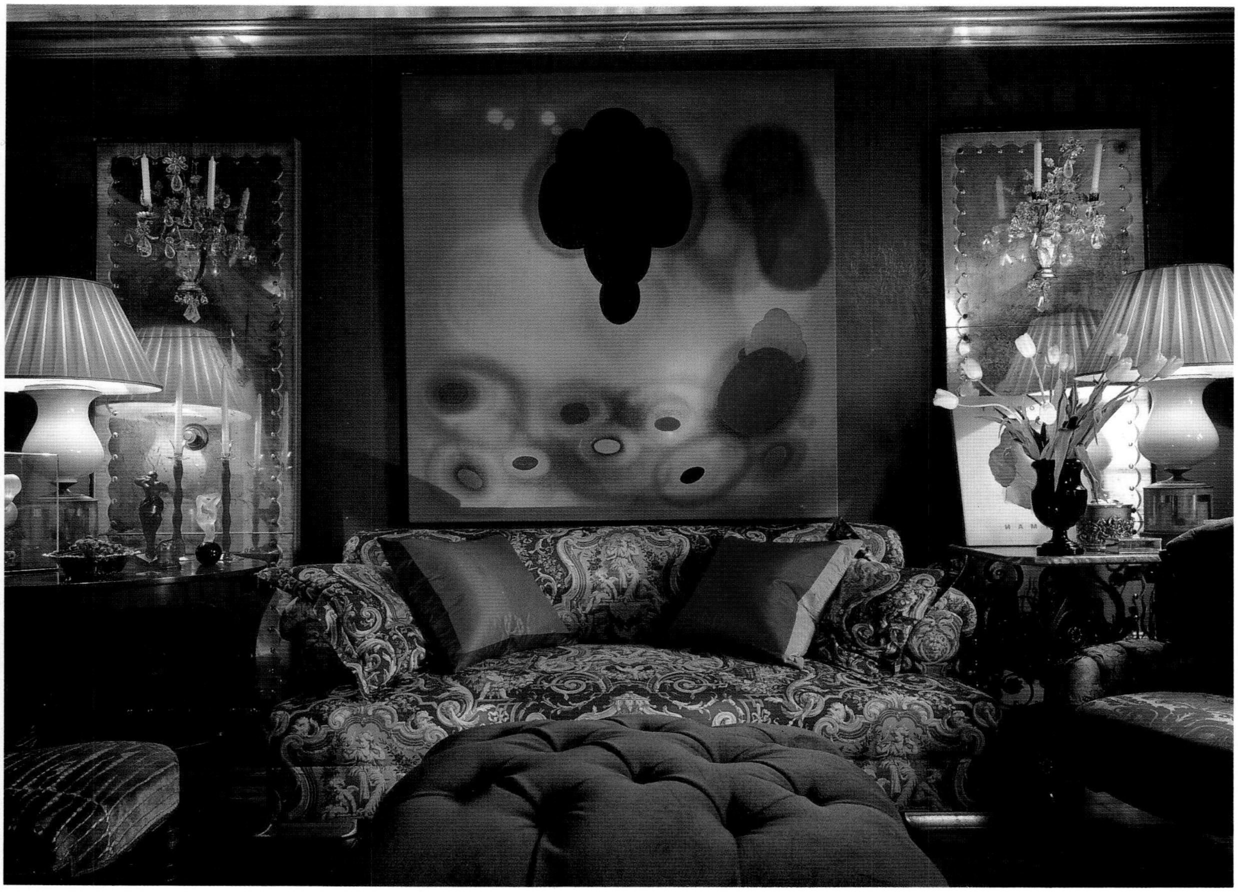

(right) This eclectic living room was designed to highlight the client's collection of Oriental antiques.

INTERIOR DESIGN
Arlis Ede Interiors, Inc.

(opposite page) Deep reds and blues accented by royal gold tones envelope a stately study.

INTERIOR DESIGN
William R. Eubanks Interior Design

(above) Hand-painted seafoam-blue stripes add a touch of whimsy to a formal entry foyer. The designer's favorite antique pink luster adds color to a demilune console.

INTERIOR DESIGN
Elizabeth Read Weber, ASID, LLC

(top right) A combination library and formal family room offers a palette inspired by the 1930s Morharjean Sarouk rug. The custom cherry woodwork creates a warm and inviting living area.

INTERIOR DESIGN
Julie Lanterman Interior Designs

(bottom right) This room was originally a music room. It no longer hears the sound of a piano, but it is a cheerful, engulfing room done in toile, colonial blue, and gingham, mixed with sunlight. A great room to daydream in.

INTERIOR DESIGN
Alexis E. Benné Interiors

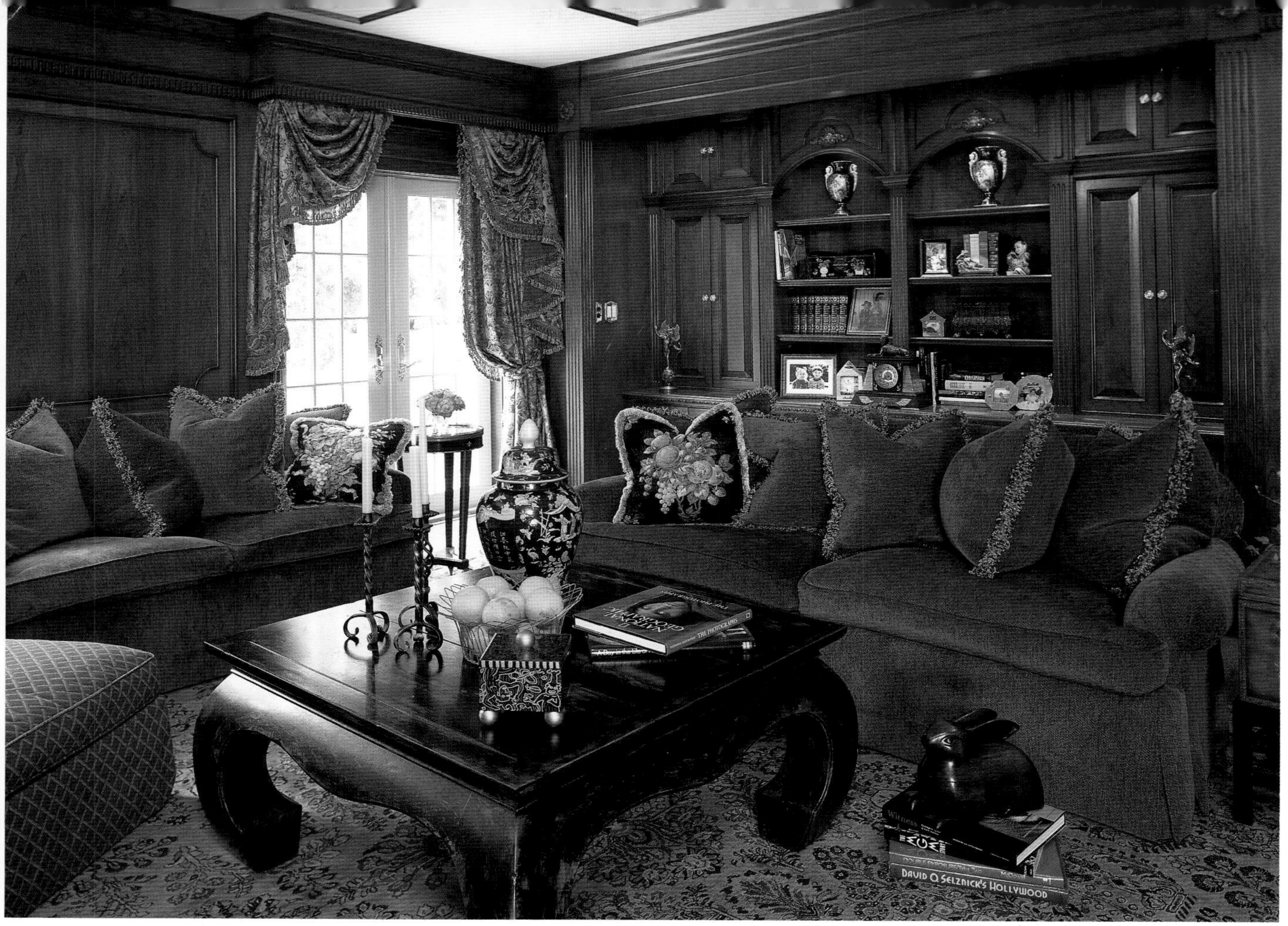
DAVID O SELZNICK'S HOLLYWOOD

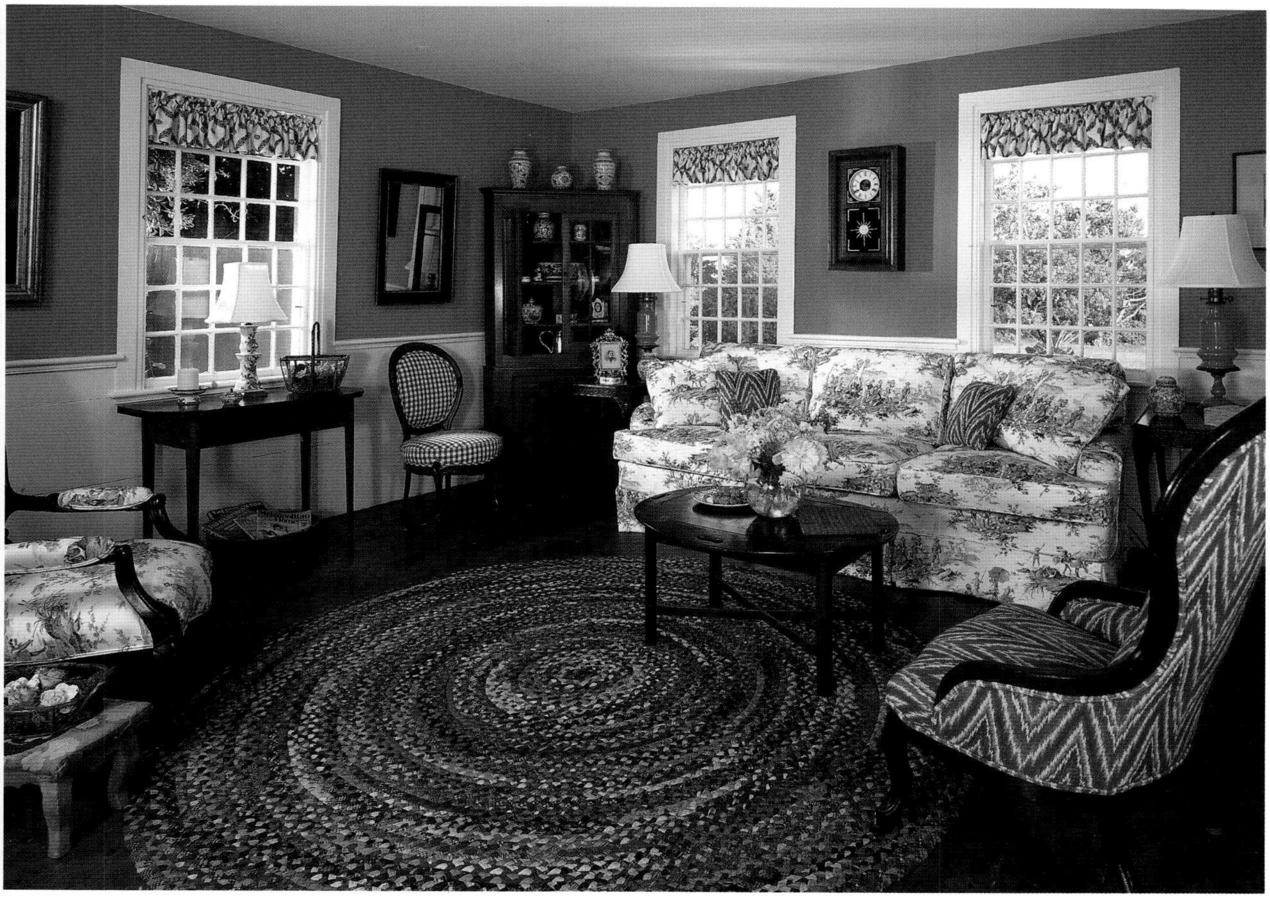

(below) Vibrant crayon colors electrify this living room, helping to brighten a home situated in a canyon.

INTERIOR DESIGN
Tomar Lampert Associates

(right) Blue glazed walls and taffeta lined organdy curtains provide a soothing backdrop to this bedroom where old and new come together.

INTERIOR DESIGN
Barbara Lazarus

(above) An exercise and entertainment area for a home sports
center boasts every possible
amenity, from a full-sized billiard
table to a private massage
room.

INTERIOR DESIGN
Horne International Designs, Inc.

Old World 17th century
Mediterranean style living
room combining all countries
and cultures.

INTERIOR DESIGN
Fetzer's Interiors

(right) INTERIOR DESIGN

William R. Eubanks Interior Design

(right) INTERIOR DESIGN

Meadowbank Designs Inc.

(left) IDeep copper and regal blue complement the wood paneling and percelain in this music room.

INTERIOR DESIGN
Akins and Aylesworth, Ltd.

(right) The grand living room of a Hudson River property projects designer Barbara Ostrom's ability to recreate period architecture, cabinetry, columns and mouldings while orchestrating color, texture, fabrics, and furnishings in a large scale setting.

INTERIOR DESIGN
Barbara Ostrom Associates

(left) Traditional New Orleans
Garden District formal parlor.

INTERIOR DESIGN
Fetzer's Interiors

(above) The designer worked with Gauguin-like colors such as greens, purples, and marigolds to provide a sheltered environment for this glass and limestone pavilion-like space. Softly upholstered cushioning on a platform became the dividing space between the living room. The contemporary, oriental design creates casual elegance.

INTERIOR DESIGN
Rita St. Clair Associates, Inc.

(above) INTERIOR DESIGN

Robert Pope Associates, Inc.

(left and below) INTERIOR DESIGN

G. M. Doveikis & Associates, Inc.

Photo: Fentress Photography

(above) Intelligent furniture
placement creates a number
of distinct functional areas in
a visually intriguing space.

INTERIOR DESIGN
Susan Fredman & Associates, Ltd.

(left and below) In a room that reverberates with color and youthful energy, an antique sideboard's lean, well-defined look harmonizes with clean-lined contemporary furniture. The sideboard's lack of applied molding is typical of the Federal era.

INTERIOR DESIGN
Marcia Connors and Roxy Gray, Growing Spaces

Photo: Steve Vierra

(above) A glass-top table with
an antique pierced stone sculpture set on a large hammered
copper vase is the focal point of
this breakfast room.

INTERIOR DESIGN
Arlis Ede Interiors, Inc.

(left) An odd shaped room lacking any architectural features was transformed into an eclectic retreat for a world traveler by the design and addition of arches, beams, corbels, and an antique French limestone fireplace. The awkwardly proportional window was enhanced into a focal point by the custom designed Palladian arched shutter treatment.

INTERIOR DESIGN

Barbara Ostrom Associates

(left) For young clients with a collection of very strong twentieth-century paintings, the objective was to achieve clarity of line and simplicity of form by using early nineteenth and twentieth century furniture with simple material.

INTERIOR DESIGN

Brian J. McCarthy, Inc.

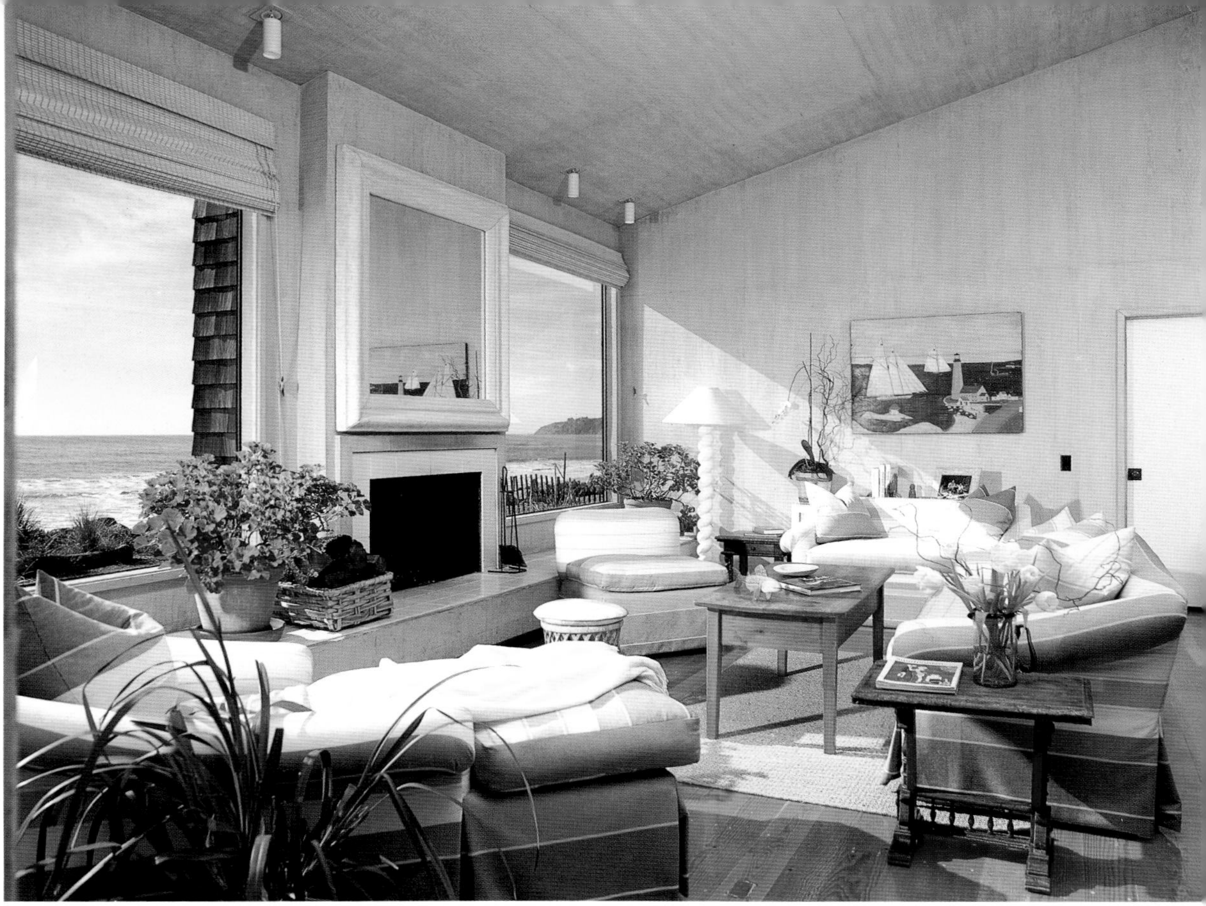

(above) INTERIOR DESIGN

Douglas Associates, Inc.

Photo: David Livingston

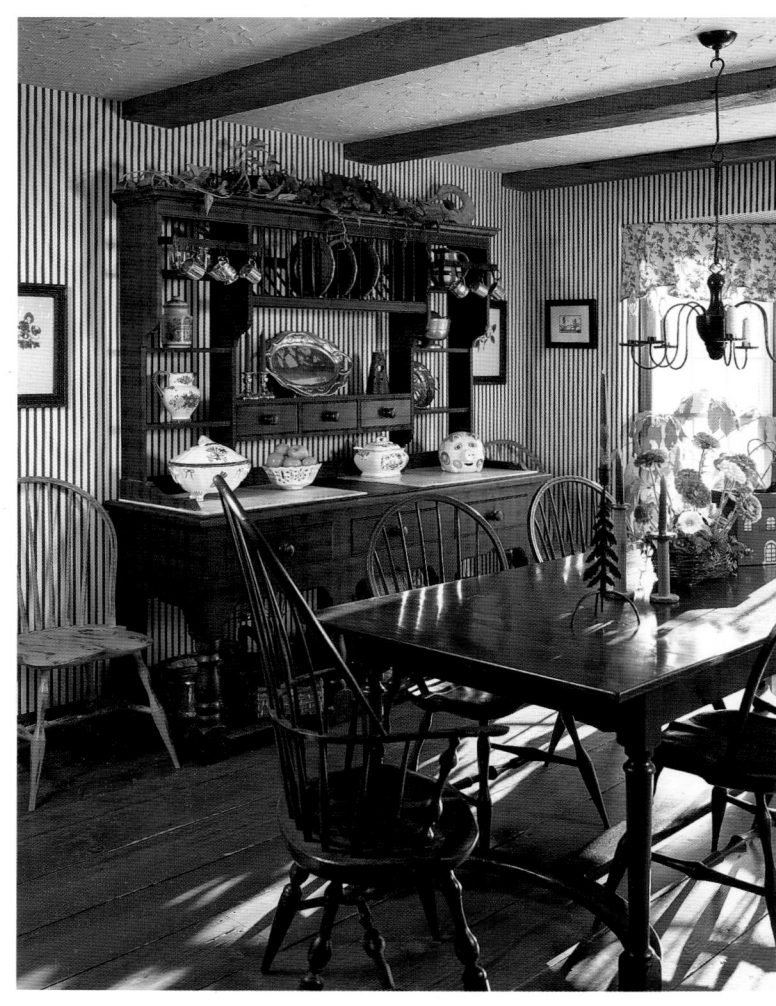

(right) Wide antique floor boards with distressed charm, handmade Windsor chairs (available through Lynn Robinson Interiors) and an old hutch in a hand-painted soft plaid breakfast room is cozy with a dressed-down sophistication.

INTERIOR DESIGN

Lynn Robinson Interiors

(above) Classic seaside charm in a
breakfast room with blue and white
sunflower fabric-covered walls and
a black Portuguese needlepoint rug
decorated with fruit and flowers.

INTERIOR DESIGN
Diamond Barratta Design, Inc.

(right) INTERIOR DESIGN

Arlene Semel & Associates, Inc.

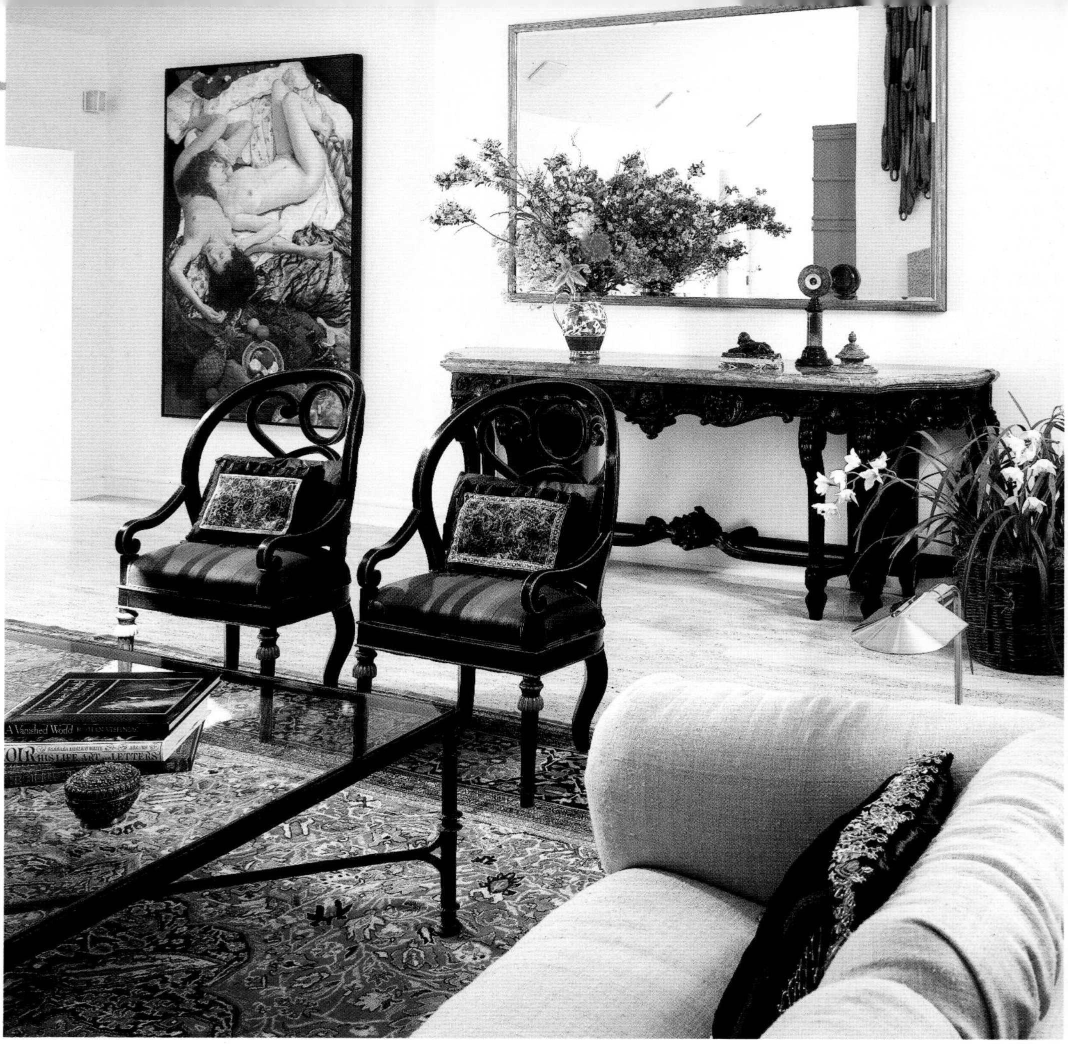

(right) A custom contemporary limestone fireplace pays homage to traditional details and serves as an anchor for the dramatic Bruce Brainard painting.

INTERIOR DESIGN

Gandy/Peace, Inc.

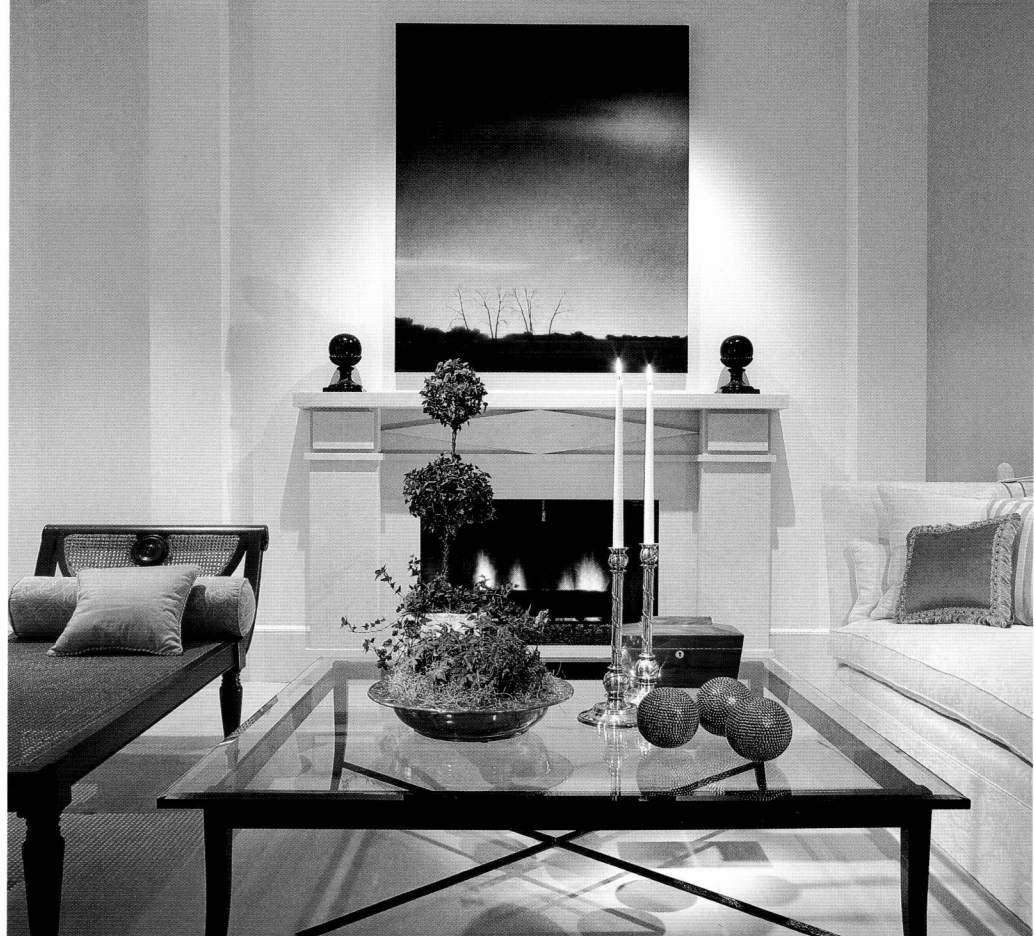

(above) INTERIOR DESIGN

Noha & Associates

Photo: Jon Miller, Hedrich Blessing

(above) A custom glass, lucite
and marble table enhances this
elegant dining room.

INTERIOR DESIGN

Fran Murphy & Associates

Photo: Rob Katanis

(right) Old World tile enlivens a
small flower sink.

INTERIOR DESIGN

Henry Johnstone & Co.

(above) Ceiling beams from an
old barn, darkly stained wood
blinds, and antiqued tile floor
and blue cabinets recreate the
look of a spacious Normandy
farmhouse kitchen. In the background is a nineteenth-century
French, authentic signed
Horloge tall case clock.

INTERIOR DESIGN
Meadowbank Designs Inc.

(left) This fully functional home office is tucked into the corner of a family room. The monitor is recessed into the wall, the printer is closeted underneath, the computer and disks are in the cabinet on the right, and the keyboard and mouse pad fold into the drawer. Everything is instantly accessible—and easily concealed.

(below) Featured on the September '95 cover of *House Beautiful*, this cheerful kitchen and family room are furnished for flexibility. Antique cabinets conceal the refrigerator (left background). *Reprinted by permission from* House Beautiful, *copyright © September 1995. The Heart Corporation. All rights reserved.*

INTERIOR DESIGN

Nancy Mullan, ASID, CKD

Photographer: Richard Felber

(above) Cool, aquatic themes recur throughout this beachside residence, rendering the mood peaceful and the aesthetics powerful.

INTERIOR DESIGN

Eberlein Design Consultants Ltd.

(left) INTERIOR DESIGN

Muriel Hebert, Inc.

Photo: John Vaughan

(below) INTERIOR DESIGN

Muriel Hebert, Inc.

Photo: Jay Graham

(right) Octagonal, turreted ceiling transforms a breakfast room from the practical to the entertaining. A space designed for warm welcomes, with white-washed oak ceiling and cabinetry in play with porcelain and the custom lead glass.

INTERIOR DESIGN
Diane Wendell Interior Design

(left) Generously proportioned
French doors invite the outdoors
to share in the casual comfort of
a cozy sun room.

INTERIOR DESIGN
Carol R. Knott Interior Design

(left) A new kitchen and pantry
was designed with a colonial
revival feeling for a stately
Westchester home.

INTERIOR DESIGN

Diamond Barratta Design, Inc.

(above) In this penthouse dining
room, the screens are adapted
from originals on the Cotê
d'Azur, the sconces are from
Old Palm Beach, the chandelier
is nineteenth-century French, and
the art is by Julian Schnabel.

INTERIOR DESIGN
Barbara Lazarus

(left) A small dining room is visually enlarged with a new bay window and rich blue color on the walls and custom rug. A lovely floral border defines the doorways and walls. The elaborately detailed window treatment adds a formal touch, while echoing the lightness of the chair fabrics. Each piece of china and stemware was painstakingly chosen to repeat the colors.

INTERIOR DESIGN
Susie Leader Interiors, Inc.

(left) Through the use of antique baskets, European wall tiles, and original barn beams, a commodious kitchen with the charm of a European country cottage was created for an active family.

INTERIOR DESIGN
Meadowbank Designs Inc.

(right) INTERIOR DESIGN
Akins and Aylesworth, Ltd.

(below) The design for this New York City dining room addresses the client's love for dramatic and vigorous entertaining. The wall and curtain colors originate in the antique tabriz carpet. The walls are glazed in a navy blue cross-hatched pattern and lacquered to a high gloss finish that reflects a candlelit room.

INTERIOR DESIGN
David Ripp Incorporated

(above) A magnificent dining
room set for dessert invites one
to relax in soft pink tones. A
regal frieze at the ceiling
enhances the room.

INTERIOR DESIGN
James R. Irving, ASID

215

(below) A painting from realist Mary Sims enhances a John's Island (Florida) residence.

INTERIOR DESIGN

Rodgers Menzies Interior Design

Photo: Rob Katanis

(right) The custom-designed table and chair play off the fabric on the seat pads. A blue arch frames the breakfast area and adds a degree of intensity.

INTERIOR DESIGN

Gail Adams Interiors Ltd.

(left) Timeless elegance marks a dining room that incorporates antique urns on the table to create balance and harmony.

INTERIOR DESIGN

Maha Jano Interiors

(above) Arresting sapphire blue
provides the foundation for a
regal dining room where inlaid
marble harmonizes with silver
leaf and weathered metal.

INTERIOR DESIGN
Eberlein Design Consultants Ltd.

(above) This triad scheme using tints of primary colors is a case study in color harmony. The values are relatively equal; no single color is more dominant than another: Because blue, yellow, and red are equidistant on the color wheel, this combination of tints is soothing but quietly enlivening as well.

Photo: Steve Vierra

(above) Good color pairings can often be taken straight from nature. Here, peach and green bring a balance of warm and cool notes to a sunny room.

Bedroom by Cassina

(right) INTERIOR DESIGN
In-Site Design Group Inc.

(above) INTERIOR DESIGN

Bedroom by B & B Italia

(right) A cobalt blue Santa Fe motif accents the gray stucco walls of a small bath. The bump-out lavatory with recessed base allows for ample storage without taking up half the room. Sophisticated touches to an otherwise whimsical theme are added through the ceramic tile border in the shower and custom chrome hardware.

INTERIOR DESIGN
Jackie Naylor Interiors, Inc.

(right) The mix of checked, plaid and floral prints in this bedroom work together because they share blue colors of the same value and saturation.

INTERIOR DESIGN
Brunschwig & Fils

(above) With its exuberant fluidity, tropical botanical fabric maintains a crispness that works well with the time-honored styling of the chairs and lamps. The fabric design is by Josef Frank, one of the founders of Swedish Modernism.

Photo courtesy of Brunschwig & Fils

White, by definition, is the combination of all colors. That is why, perhaps, it is the best complement to every color imaginable. White will stay cool and bright, both day and night. The clean, crisp feeling of a white room is unmatched by any other color. White is chameleon-like because of its reflective properties: It shines on its own, or can reflect other color in the room to create a soft, colored glow. It is the perfect background for showcasing a prize piece of art, a stunning couch, an intricately patterned rug. White recedes and allows architectural elements to hold their own instead of competing with color. Not only the perfect background, it is the perfect accent. Add white accents to a room full of color so that the eyes can rest. It can help create a soft, weathered look that is inviting. The classic pairing of white and black in a room will add drama to any room. From cool white linen in a bedroom to soft, cloud-like couches in a living room, white can be found everywhere in the home.

(right) Details abound in the
sweeping proportions of this
carefully accented living area.

INTERIOR DESIGN
Kuckly Associates, Inc.

(right) A greenhouse "folly,"
abundant in architectural
details and exotic furnishings.
Built off site and hoisted to the
8th floor terrace of a New
York City brownstone.

INTERIOR DESIGN
Barbara Ostrom Associates, Inc.

(above) The unifying elements of cherry and
limestone create a "furniture" look for this round
kitchen and adjacent family room. The down-filled
banquette, cherry drink ledge, custom table (with
one side open for remotes), and a collection of
antique photos make this a warm and inviting
center for relaxed living.

INTERIOR DESIGN

Gandy/Peace, Inc.

(left and below) INTERIOR DESIGN

Robert Stilin, Inc.

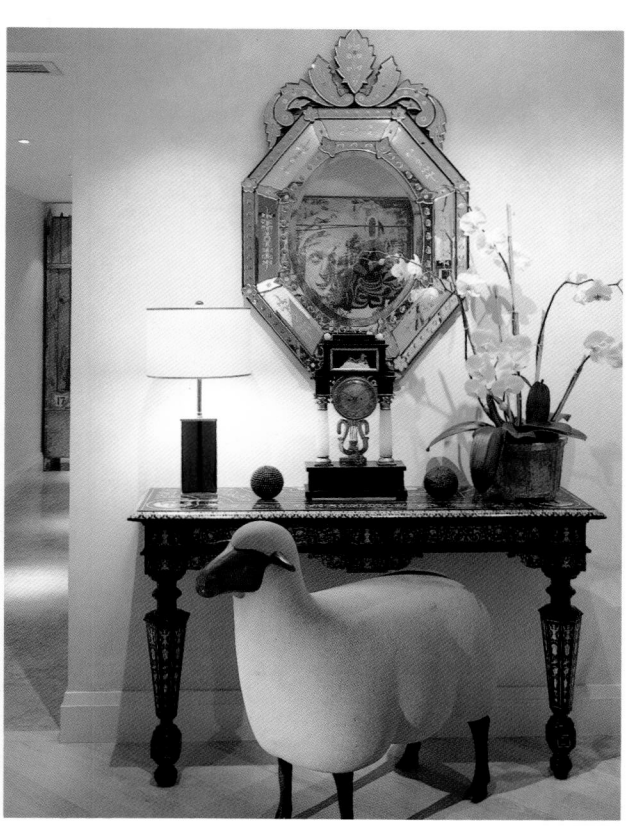

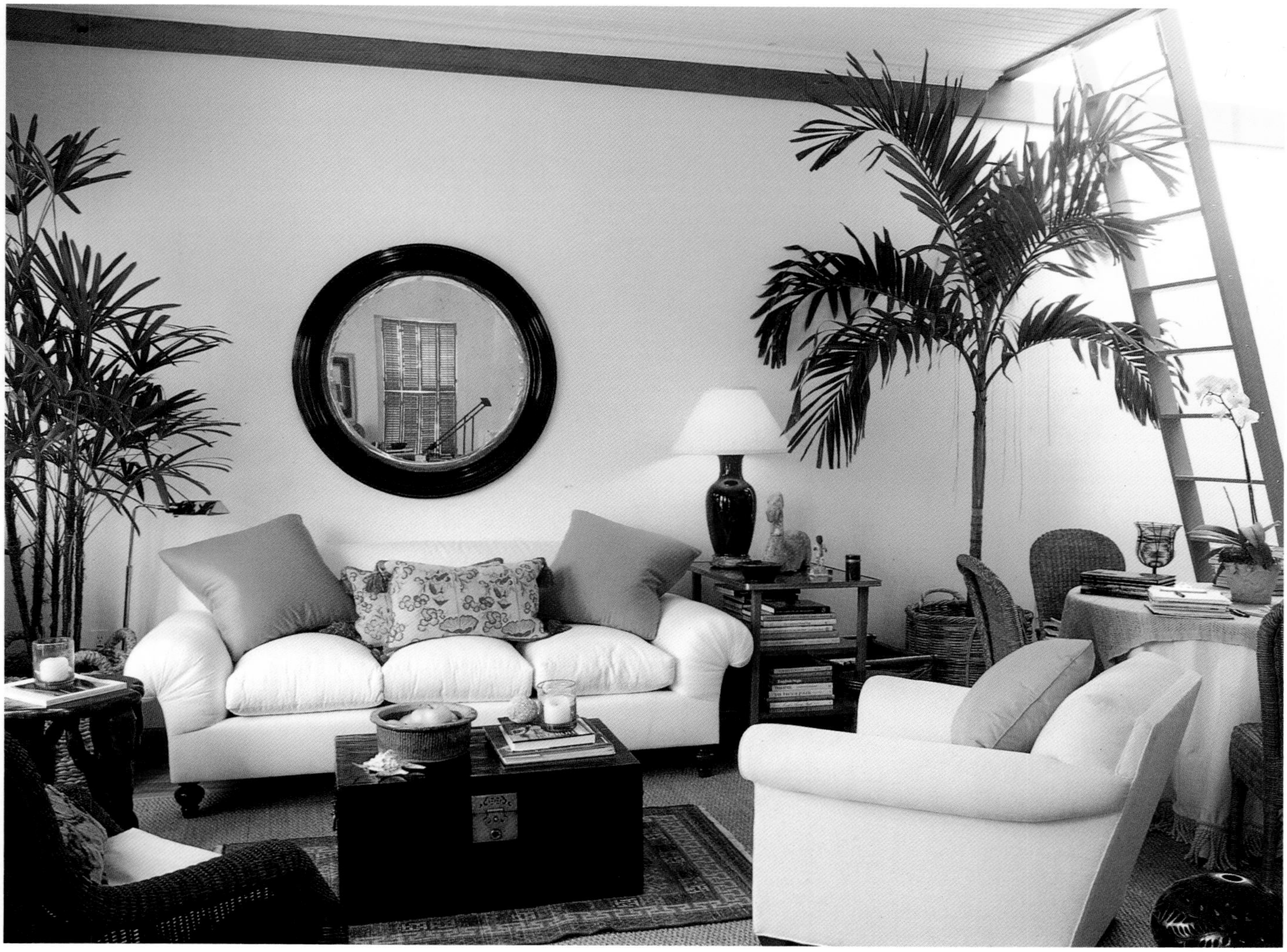

(above) Texture is the key word in this comfortable, but subtle, informal living space. Diverse fabrics complement the sisal flooring and underscore the richness of the antique Chinese bamboo underwear, which is mounted on a custom cherry rod with bronze finials.

INTERIOR DESIGN

Gandy/Peace, Inc.

(right) Stones found on the homeowner's property inspired the color palette in this comfortable space.

INTERIOR DESIGN

Gail Adams Interiors Ltd.

(below) INTERIOR DESIGN

Joan Spiro Interiors

(above) INTERIOR DESIGN

Robert Stilin, Inc.

(above) INTERIOR DESIGN

Environmental Images by Marilyn Lundy

(right) This living room features a light hand-rubbed finish breakfront with a shell motif pediment. The breakfront provides a focal point for the conversation group of soft seating pieces upholstered in light pastels accentuating the bright, casually elegant appearance of the house.

INTERIOR DESIGN

Pedlar's Village Interior Designs

(above) INTERIOR DESIGN

VanTosh & Associates

Photo: Mike Moreland

(left) The great outdoors comes inside through this garden-room addition.

INTERIOR DESIGN

Fran Murphy & Associates

(right) A stunning gold-leaf coffered
ceiling is the centerpiece of this
transitional living room.

INTERIOR DESIGN

Designworks Creative Partnership, Ltd.

(below) Beige chenille upholstery and iron floor lamps with parchment shades contribute to the casual elegance of a Malibu living room.

INTERIOR DESIGN
Ron Wilson Designer

(above) Custom furniture designs for sofa, chairs, coffee tables, end tables, wood screen and projection chandelier. Custom fabric treatments on columns, custom light trough, custom modular wall finish. (Custom furniture fabrication by Barry Salechian)

INTERIOR DESIGN

Michael C. F. Chan & Associates, Inc.

(above) Off-white furnishings contrast with
dark tables and the pinao in the background
to achieve a look of casual elegance.

INTERIOR DESIGN
Kuckly Associates, Inc.

(above) INTERIOR DESIGN

Ruth Livingston Interior Design

Photo: Dennis Anderson

(above) Responding to the client's
taste—which favored a neutral,
"timeless" palette—the designer
used clean-lined, classic upholstered
pieces with a mix of oriental fabrics
and ethnic accessories.

INTERIOR DESIGN
Walker Design Group

(left) Sharp contrast and eclectic
design elements intensify a grand
entry and living room.

INTERIOR DESIGN
Designworks Creative Partnership, Ltd.

(right) Contemporary elegance permeates this president's office. The desk is crafted of Carpathian elm burl.

(below) Antique accents and contemporary art provide numerous focal points in this divided living room.

INTERIOR DESIGN

Designworks Creative Partnership, Ltd.

(above) A sensuous textural delight provided
by hand-woven casement draperies, along
with silks, leather, tapestry, marble, wood, steel
and glass, gives this bachelor's living room a
strong sense of individual style.

INTERIOR DESIGN

Pedlar's Village Interior Design

(above) INTERIOR DESIGN

M. L. Slovack Design, Inc.

(right) A massive antique pool table with inlaid and carved detailing provides visual ballast in an open-concept house with soaring volumes of space.

INTERIOR DESIGN

Rita St. Clair

Photo: Deborah Mazzoleni

(left and above) INTERIOR DESIGN

Est Est, Inc.

(left) Photo: Mark Boisclair

(above) Photo: Tony Hernandez

(above) INTERIOR DESIGN

Gail Adams Interiors Ltd.

Photo: Mark Boisclair·

(right) Green and white slipcovers
help create an expression of summer
in this seasonal living room.

INTERIOR DESIGN

Ron Hefler

(above) INTERIOR DESIGN

Carol Conway Design Associates

Photo: Mark Boisclair

(above) The Oriental screen and black-and-white striped Empire-style chairs from Spain are in perfect accord with the neutral color scheme, which is a constant in this high-rise condominium.

INTERIOR DESIGN

Lloy Hack Associates

Photo: Steve Rosenthal

(above) Residence at Williams Island.

INTERIOR DESIGN

JoyCe Stolberg Interiors, Inc.

(above) Comfortable seating and tapestry fabrics create an environment of casual living enhanced further by the rusty-red textured coffee table. Note how honey tones and washed wood mix in the entertainment center.

INTERIOR DESIGN

Pat Stotler Interiors, Inc.

(this page) INTERIOR DESIGN
In-Site Design Group Inc.

(above) A fireplace defines the space, while custom shelving gives variety and texture to the walls.

INTERIOR DESIGN

Michael C. F. Chan & Associates, Inc.

(above) INTERIOR DESIGN

Arlene Semel & Associates, Inc.

(right) INTERIOR DESIGN

Douglas Associates, Inc.

Photo: Mark Sinclair

(above) Sparkling white and subtle gray add to the expansive feeling of this lofty architecture. Glistening brass and glass work well with the block patterned fabric and contemporary art. The impact is heightened by the informally balanced draperies.

INTERIOR DESIGN
Linda Glantz Interiors Ltd.

(above) Provides intimate areas to allow
entertaining for one couple or seventy people.
The room centers around the fireplace but also
provides for a built-in service bar, game area,
and second conversation area.

INTERIOR DESIGN

Peter Charles Interiors

(above) Vibrant, rich colors
provide a beautiful contrast
to a contemporary, neutral
background.

INTERIOR DESIGN
Gail Adams Interiors Ltd.

(left) INTERIOR DESIGN
Carol Conway Design Associates

Photo: Mark Boisclair

(above) Designed for a professional football
player, this casual media room features a
custom video cabinet with room for showcasing helmets from current and former
teams.

INTERIOR DESIGN

Gail Adams Interiors Ltd.

(right) INTERIOR DESIGN

Gail Adams Interiors Ltd

(above) Artwork and fabrics in this
contemporary living room rely on the
rich palette of the Southwest.

INTERIOR DESIGN
Gail Adams Interiors Ltd.

(right) Soaring above the room, a mirror
with classical themes gains prominence
through its placement.

INTERIOR DESIGN
Bierly-Drake Associates

Photo: Sam Gray

(above) A careful mix of antiques characterizes this 1920s Spanish home. Highlights include the antique English Bible box next to the chair and an old English coffer is used as an end table.

INTERIOR DESIGN
Carol Wolk Interiors Ltd.

(right) Vanilla-colored silk sofas and down-filled chairs face an iron cocktail table displaying brushed pewter candlesticks and an Italian porcelain swan.

INTERIOR DESIGN
Pat Stotler Interiors Inc.

(left) The bedroom was designed for the ASID Phoenix Showcase house. The setting was a newly constructed "sixteenth century French chateau" with a view overlooking a pond.

INTERIOR DESIGN
Walker Design Group

(opposite page) A limestone fireplace and inviting overstuffed furniture complement the neutral background in a Bel-Air living room.

INTERIOR DESIGN
Ron Wilson Designer

(above) Understated elegance is achieved
with gleaming white floors and walls that
enhance the owner's colorful art and glass
collection.

INTERIOR DESIGN
Carrie Brockman's Design Group

(right) INTERIOR DESIGN
Lowrance Interiors, Inc.

(left) Timeless accessories bring a serene quality to a setting that celebrates the natural environment.

INTERIOR DESIGN

Sistine Interiors

(above) In an elegant hall of a contemporary residence, each furnishing item is surrounded by ample space. As a result, antiques as well as whimsical new art furniture take on the commanding quality of objects in a gallery.

INTERIOR ARCHITECTURE

Olson Lewis & Dioli Architects

Photo: Eric Roth

(above) A greenhouse "folly," abundant in
architectural details and exotic furnishings. Built
off site and hoisted to the 8th floor terrace of a
New York City brownstone.

INTERIOR DESIGN

Barbara Ostrom Associates, Inc.

An eclectic mix of periods and ideas that range
from a drop-leaf table found at a yard sale to a
hand-woven linen rug creates a comfortable and
inviting living room.

INTERIOR DESIGN
Vicente Wolf Associates

(above) INTERIOR DESIGN

James R. Irving, ASID

(above) INTERIOR DESIGN

Lowrance Interiors, Inc.

(above) INTERIOR DESIGN

Blair Design Associates, Inc.

(above) INTERIOR DESIGN

Mark Weaver & Associates

Photo: John Vaughan

(above) Bright white cabinetry, brass drawer
pulls, and checkerboard tiles keep things light
and airy in this diminutive 12 foot x 12 foot
(3.6 meter x 3.6 meter) country kitchen.

INTERIOR DESIGN

Diane Alpern Kovacs Interior Design, Inc.

(above) INTERIOR DESIGN

Ruth Livingston Interior Design

Photo: John Vaughan

(above) The dining room is enhanced by
silver leaf, a detail that creates a light,
reflecting ambience suitable for both day
and evening entertaining.

INTERIOR DESIGN
Justin Sancho Interior Design, Ltd.

(right) INTERIOR DESIGN
Leslie Jones, Inc.

(above) The magnificent base of the dining room table brings a distinct Oriental flavor to this residence. The chairs are in the style of Chippendale, who drew heavily on Chinese design.

INTERIOR DESIGN
Anne Tarasoff Interiors

Photo: Bill Rothschild

(above) INTERIOR DESIGN

NDM Kitchens, Inc.

(above) A 500-gallon salt water fish tank
seduces diners to linger in this contemporary
space.

INTERIOR DESIGN
Carrie Brockman's Design Group

(above) A large white paper lantern by
Swedish designer, Ingo Mauer, becomes the
centerpiece of the dining area in this contemporary California hilltop home. The neutral
color pallette is set against pure white walls,
includes pale natural linen drapery fabric,
clear beechwood furniture and natural sisal
floorcovering. With details left to a minimum,
the story for this room is about shape and the
use of pale colors.

INTERIOR DESIGN
David Dalton Associates

(above) A live-in kitchen in an 1890's ocean-front
"cottage" had to be stripped down to the studs due
to a previous design "makeover" in the 1970's—
complete with harvest gold Formica counters and
acoustical tile ceilings. The challenge: making the
large state-of-the-art kitchen convenient for one chef
or several—and in keeping with the period of the
house.

INTERIOR DESIGN
Stedila Design Inc.

Akins & Aylesworth, Ltd.
26 E. First Street Hinsdale, IL 60521
630/325.3355
Fax: 630/325.3315

Al Evans Interiors
1001 South Bayshore Drive, #2902
Miami, FL 33131

Alexis E. BennÈ Interiors
100 Riverside Drive
New York, NY 10024
212/580.8118
Fax: 212/769.0809

Ann Platz & Company
Five Piedmont Center, Suite 202
Atlanta, GA 30305
404/237.1000
Fax: 404/237.3810

Anne Tarasoff Interiors
25 Andover Road
Port Washington, NY 11050

Anne Weinberg Designs, Inc.
982 Chestnut Run
Gates Mills, OH 44040
440/423.0443
Fax: 440/423.0443

Antine Associates
1028 Arcadian Way
Fort Lee, NJ 07024
201/941.8048

Arlene Semel & Associates, Inc.
445 N. Franklin
Chicago, IL 60610
312/644.1480
Fax: 312/644.8157
e-mail: asasemel@aol.com

Arlis Ede Interiors, Inc.
3520 Fairmount
Dallas, TX 75219
214/521.1302
Fax: 214/559.4729

B & B Italia, USA, Inc.
150 East 58th Street
Architects and Designers Building
New York, NY 10155

Barbara Jacobs Interior Design
12340 Saratoga-Sunnyvale Road
Saratoga, CA 95070
408/446.2225
Fax: 408/446.2607

Barbara Lazarus
10 Fones Alley
Providence, RI 02906
401/521.8910
Fax: 401438.8809

Barbara Metzler Interior Design, Inc.
120 Woodley Road
Winnetka, IL 60093
847/501.2929
Fax: 847/501.2923

Barbara Ostrom Associates
One International Plaza
Mahwah, NJ 07495
201/529.0444
Fax: 201/529.0449
and
55 East 87th Street
New York NY 10128
212/465.1808

Barry Dixon, Inc.
2019 Q Street, NW
Washington, DC 20009
202/332.7955
Fax: 202/332.7952

Bierly-Drake Associates, Inc.
17 Arlington Street
Boston, MA 02116

Blair Design Associates
315 West 78th Street
New York, NY10024
212/595.0203
Fax: 212/595.0245
e-mail: blairdesign@msn.com

Bobbi Packer Designs
126 Edgecliffe Drive
Highland Park, IL 60035
847/432.0407
Fax: 847/432.0490

Brian J. McCarthy, Inc.
1414 Avenue of the Americas, Suite 404
New York, NY 10019
212/308.7600
Fax: 212/308.4242

Brown's Interiors, Inc.
1115 Kenilworth Avenue
Charlotte, NC 28204
704/375.2248
Fax: 704/334.0982

Brunschwig & Fils
979 Third Avenue
New York, NY 10022

Busch and Associates
1615 N. Mohawk
Chicago, IL 60614
312/649.9106
Fax: 312/649.9106

C.M. Wright, Inc.
700 N. La Cienega Boulevard
Los Angeles, CA 90069
310/657.7655
Fax: 310/657.4440

C. Weaks Interiors, Inc.
3391 Habersham Road
Atlanta, GA 30305
404/233.6040
Fax: 404/233.6043

Carl Steele Associates
1606 Pine Street
Philadelphia, PA 19103
215/546.5530
Fax: 215/546.1571

Carol Conway Design Associates
8242 E. Del Codena
Scottsdale, AZ 85258
602/948.1959
Fax: 602/948.1959

Carol R. Knott Interior Design
430 Green Bay Road
Kenilworth, IL 60043
847/256.6676
Fax: 847/256.6689

Carol Wolk Interiors, Ltd.
340 Tudor Court
Glencoe, IL 60022
847/835.5500
Fax: 847/835.0309

Carrie Brockman's Design Group
322 North Meramac
Clayton, OH 63105
314/726.6333
Fax: 314/721.0778

Cassina USA
200 McKay Road
Huntington Station, NY 11746

Chambers Interiors and Associates, Inc.
2719 Laclede, Suite B
Dallas, TX 75204
214/871.9222
Fax: 214/871.0644

Clara Hayes Barrett Designs
300 Boylston Street
Boston, MA 022116
617/426.6144
Fax: 617/426.6415

Claude Guidi
411 East 57th Street
New York, NY 10022

Clifford Stiles McAlpin Interiors, Inc.
900 East Moreno Street
Pensacola, FL 32503
850/438.8345
Fax: 850/434.8315

Coulson-Hamlin
2838 Bellefontaine
Houston, TX 77025
713/666.1620
Fax: 713/666.2410

Creative Decorating
168 Poloke Place
Honolulu, HI.96822
808/955.1465
Fax: 808/943.8450

Cricket Interiors
2505 Arlington Road
Cleveland Heights, OH 44118
216/321.5087
Fax: 216/321.9035
e-mail: helldeg@aol.com

Dakota Jackson
979 Third Avenue, Suite 503
New York, NY 10022

David Dalton Associates
8687 Melrose Avenue, Suite G290
Los Angeles, CA 90069
310/289.6010
Fax: 310/289.6011

David Ripp Incorporated
215 West 84th Street
New York, NY 10024
212/362.7706
Fax: 212/362.4486
e-mail: dugancastle@worldnet.att.net

David Webster & Associates
254 W. 25th Street
New York, NY 10001
212/924.8932
Fax: 212/477.3934

Dennis Rolland Inc.
405 East 54th Street
New York, NY 10022
212/644.0537
Fax: 212/486.9189

Designworks Creative Partnership, Ltd.
6501 Park of Commerce Boulevard
Boca Raton, FL 33487
561/912.9860
Fax: 561/912.9865

Deutsch/Parker Design, Ltd.
325 West Huron Street, Suite 500
Chicago, IL 60610
312/649.1244
Fax: 312/649.9617

Diamond Baratta Design Inc.
270 Lafayette Street
New York, NY 10012
212/966.8892
Fax: 212/966.4261

Diane Alpern Kovacs, Interior Design, Inc.
4 Main Street
Roslyn, NY 11576
516/625.0703
Fax: 516/625.8441
e-mail: cottagered@aol.com

Diane Wendell Interior Design
1121 Warren Avenue
Downers Grove, IL 60515
630/852.0235
Fax: 630/988.8341

Dorothy H. Travis Interiors, Inc.
12 Kings Circle, NE
Atlanta, GA, 30305
404/233.7210
Fax: 404/233.7260

Douglas Associates, Inc.
2525 E. Exposition Avenue
Denver, CO 80209
303/722.6979
Fax: 303/722.9663

Eberlein Design Consultants, Ltd.
1809 Walnut Street, Suite 410
Philadelphia, PA 19103
215/405.0400
Fax: 215/405.0588

Edward C. Turrentine Interior Design, Inc.
70 N. Raymond Avenue
Pasadena, CA 91103
626/795.9964
or
213/681.4221
Fax: 626/795.0027

Elaine Bass Interiors
11 Rutland Road
Great Neck, NY 11020
516/482.6834
Fax: 516/482.7138

Elizabeth Read Weber, LLC
79 East Putnam Avenue
Greenwich, CT 06830
203/869.5659
Fax: 203/869.3778
e-mail: erwllc@aol.com

Ellen Lemer Korney Associates
10170 Culver Boulevard
Culver City, CA 90232
310/204.6576
Fax: 310/204.1457

Ellen Sosnow Interiors
850 Park Avenue
New York, NY 10021
212/744.0214
Fax: 212/772.3443

Environments by Marilyn Frances Lundy
One Lincoln Plaza, Suite 305
New York, NY 10023
212/362.7057
Fax: 212/362.7057

Est Est, Inc.
7050 Main Street
Scottsdale, AZ 85251
602/946.6555
Fax: 602/423.1093

Fetzer's Interiors
711 Jefferson Highway
Baton Rouge, LA 70806
504/927.7420
Fax: 504/927.8280

Fran Murphy & Associates
71 E. Allendale Road
Saddle River, NJ 07458
201/934.6029
Fax: 201/934.5597
e-mail: enm2@worldnet.att.net

Freya Serabian Design Associates
36 Church Street
Winchester, MA 01890

G.M. Doveikis & Associates, Inc.
2058 Concourse Drive
St. Louis, MO 63146
314/567.4944
Fax: 314/537.9629
e-mail: gmdanda@aol.com

G.S. Hinsen Company
2133 Brandywood Drive
Nashville, TN 37215
615/383.6440
Fax: 615/269.5130

Gail Adams Interiors, Ltd.
110 East San Miguel
Phoenix, AZ 85012
602/274.0074
Fax: 602/274.897

Gandy/Peace, Inc.
349 Peachtree Hills Avenue, NE,
Suite C-2
Atlanta, GA 30350
404/237.8681
Fax: 404/237.6150
e-mail: charlesgandy@mindspring.com

Gerhard Design Group
7630 El Camino Real Rancho
La Costa, CA 92009
760/436.0181
Fax: 760/435.7945

Ginny Stine Interiors
1936 Marco Boulevard
Jacksonville, FL 32207
904/396.9814
Fax: 904/398.3175

Growing Spaces
Marcia Connors & Roxy Gray
4 Fall Lane
Canton, MA 02021

Harte-Brownlee & Associates, Inc.
1691 Westcliff Drive
Newport Beach, CA 92660
714/548.9530
Fax: 714/548.9528

Henry Johnstone & Company
95 San Miguel Road
Pasadena, CA 91105
818/716.7624
Fax: 818/716.0017

Home International Designs, Inc.
5272 River Road, Suite 450
Bethesda, MD 20816
301/656.4304
Fax: 301/907.0258

Ida Goldstein
16 Munnings Drive
Sudbury, MA 01776

In-Site Design Group
3551 S. Monaco Parkway
Denver, CO 80237
303/691.9000
Fax: 303/757.6475

Interior Designs by Daphne Weiss Inc.
P.O. Box 7005
Boca Raton, FL 33431
561/392.6301
Fax: 561/395.4409
e-mail: dweiss4@IBM.net

Interior Options
200 Lexington Avenue
New York, NY 10016
212/545.0301
Fax: 212/689.4064

J. Dayvault & Associates
78 Peachtree Circle
Atlanta, GA 30309
404/873.1873
Fax: 404/873.4271
e-mail: jday@aol.com

J. Powell and Associates, Inc.
100 W. Beaver Creek Boulevard
P.O. Box 1641 Avon, CO 81620
970/845.7731
Fax: 970/845.8903
e-mail: jpowell@vail.net

J. Westerfield Antiques & Interiors, Inc.
4429 Old Canton Road
Jackson, MS 39211
601/362.7508
Fax: 601/366.4718

Jackie Naylor Interiors, Inc.
4287 Glengary Drive
Atlanta, GA 30342
404/814.1973
Fax: 404/814.1973

James R. Irving ASID
13901 Shaker Boulevard
Cleveland, OH 44120
216/283.1991
or
216/751.1100

Jane Crary Interior Design
784 Park Avenue
New York, NY 10021
212/737.5890
Fax: 212/861.3884

Jane J. Marsden Antiques & Interiors, Inc.
2300 Peachtree Road, 102A
Atlanta, GA 30309
404/355.1288
Fax: 404/355.4552

Jennifer Garrigues, Inc.
308 Peruvian Avenue
Palm Beach, FL 33480
561/659.7085
Fax: 561/659.7090

Joan Halperin/Interior Design
401 East 80th Street
New York, NY 10021
212/288.8636
Fax: 212/472.3743

Joan Spiro Interiors
P.O. Box 1170 OVS
Great Neck, NY 11023
516/829.9087
Fax: 516/829.1578

Joanne DePalma Inc.
2109 Broadway, 1570
New York, NY 10023
212/799.6088
Fax: 212/799.4014

John Henry Sherman Jr. Interiors
9615 Thomas Drive
Panama City, FL 32407
850/233.0413
Fax: 850/230.9035

John Robert Wiltgen Design
70 West Hubbard, #205
Chicago, IL 60610

Joyce Stolberg Interiors, Inc.
2205 NE 201 Street N.
Miami Beach, FL 33150
305/931.6010
Fax: 305/931.6040

Judith Lynne Interior Design
P.O. Box 4998
Palm Springs, CA 92263
760/324.7606
Fax: 760/328.8190

Julie Lanterman Interior Designs
5 St. Francis Road
Hillsborough, CA.94010
650/348.3823
Fax: 650/348.3823

Justine Sancho Interior
4827 Fairmont Avenue
Bethesda, MD 20814
301/718.8041
Fax: 301/718.3095

Kathleen Buoymaster, Inc.
6933 La Jolla Boulevard
La Jolla, CA 92037
619/456.2850
Fax: 619/456.0672

Klingmans of Grand Rapids
3525 28th Street, SE
Grand Rapids, Mi 49512
616/942.7300
Fax: 616/942.1957

Kuckly Associates
506 E. 74th Street
New York, NY 10021
212/772.2228
Fax: 212/772.2130

Kuhl Design Associates
5100 Westheimer, Suite 200
Houston, TX 77056
713/840.1500
Fax: 713/840.1318
e-mail: pekulh@aol.com

Laura Bohn Design Associates, Inc.
30 W 26 Street
New York, NY 10010
212/645.3636
Fax: 212/645.3639

Leslie Jones, Inc.
754 N. Milwaukee Avenue
Chicago, IL 60622
312/455.1147
Fax: 312/455.1264
e-mail: LJI@interaccess.com

Letelier & Rock Design, Inc.
1020 Madison
New York, NY 10021
212/988.2398
Fax: 212/683.7608

Linda Glantz Interiors, Ltd.
329 Main
Ames, IA 50010
515/232.3752
Fax: 515/232.7467

Lloy Hack Associates
425 Boylston Street
Boston, MA 02116

Lovick Design
11339 Bumham Street
Los Angeles, CA 90049

Lowrance Interiors, Inc.
707 N. Alfred Street
Los Angeles, CA 90069
213/655.9713
Fax: 213/655.0359

Lynn Robinson Interiors
Powers Building,
34 Audrey Avenue
Oyster Bay, NY 11771
615/921.4455
Fax: 615/921.8163

M. L. Slovack Design, Inc.
7610 Bryonwood
Houston, TX 77055
713/956.7240
Fax: 713/682.7184

Maha Jano Interiors
1700 Stutz, Suite 102B
Troy, MI 48084
248/816.8044
Fax: 248/647.5618

Margot S. Wilson
4305 Westover Place N.W.
Washington, DC 20016
202/244.2171
Fax: 202/363.6647

Mario Buatta Inc.
120 East 80th Street
New York, NY 10021
212/988.6811
Fax: 212/861.9321

Mark Weaver & Associates
521 N. La Cienega Boulevard
Los Angeles, CA 90048
310/855.0400
Fax: 310/855.0332
e-mail: weaverm310@aol.com

Mary W. Delaney Interior Design
1 Strawberry Hill Court
Stamford, CT 06902
203/348.6839
Fax: 203/324.7229

Meadowbank Designs, Inc.
Box 168
Bryn Mawr, PA 19010
610/525.4909
Fax: 610/525.3909

Michael C.F. Chan & Associates, Inc.
3550 W. 6th Street, PH
Los Angeles, CA 90020
213/283.2162
Fax: 213/283.1815
e-mail: MCFCA@earthlink.net

Michael deSantis, Inc.
1110 Second Avenue
New York, NY 10022
212/753.8871

Muriel Hebert Interiors
117 Sheridan Avenue
Piedmont, CA 94611
510/547.1294
Fax: 510/655.1509

Myrl Talkington Designs
6915 Tokolm
Dallas, TX 75214
214/328.9942
Fax: 214/321.4067

Nancy Mullen NDM Kitchens Inc.
204 E. 77th Street
New York, NY 10021
212/628.4629
Fax: 212/628.6738

Nicholson Interiors
1810 West 35th Street
Austin, TX 78703
512/458.6395
Fax: 512/567.2050

Noha & Associates, Inc.
1735 W. Fletcher
Chicago, IL 60657
773/549.1414
Fax: 773/549.1479

Oetgen Design Inc.
2300 Peachtree Road, NW, Suite B-209
Atlanta, GA 30309
404/352.1112
Fax: 404/352.0505

Olson Lewis & Dioli Architects
17 Elm Street
Manchester-by-the-Sea, MA 01944

Pat Stotler Interiors
6735 East Greenway Parkway
Scottsdale, AZ 85254
602/607.1934
Fax: 602/607.1935

Pedlar's Village Interior Design
3562 S. Osprey Avenue
Sarasota, FL 34239
941/955.5726
Fax: 941/366.9563

Peter Charles Associates, Ltd.
17 East Main Street
Oyster Bay, NY 11771
516/624.9276
Fax: 516/625.9367

Rhonda A. Roman Interiors
2148 Seminole
Detroit, MI 48214
313/924.6877
Fax: 313/921.9378

Ricki Tucker Interiors/Cabin Antiques
8343 Russell-Topton Road
Meridian, MS 39305
601/679.7921
Fax: 601/484.3225
or
601/679.7200
e-mail: tuck@cybertron.com

Riemenschneider Design Associates, Inc.
122 S. Main Street, Suite 355
Ann Arbor, MI 48106
313/930.0882
Fax: 313/930.0974
e-mail: alyce@riedesign.com

Rita St. Clair Associates, Inc.
1009 N. Charles Street
Baltimore, MD 21201
410/752.1313
Fax: 410/752.1335

Robert E. Tartarini Interiors
P.O. Box 293
Old Westbury, NY 11568

Robert Pope Associates, Inc.
400 N. Wells Street, #400
Chicago, IL 60610
312/527.2077
Fax: 312/527.2079
e-mail: rpopeassoc@aol.com

Robert Stilin, Inc.
292 South County Road
Palm Beach, FL 33480
561/832.8176
Fax: 561/832.8145
e-mail: robert stilin@worldnet.att.net
and
P.O. Box 4189
East Hampton, NY 11937
516/380.6542
Fax: 516/329.8932

Rodgers Menzies Interior Design
766 South White Station Road
Memphis, TN 38117
901/761.3161
Fax: 901/763.3993

Ron Hefler
465 South Sweetzer Avenue
Los Angeles, CA 90048
213/651.1231
Fax: 213/735.2502

Ron Wilson Designer, Inc.
1235 Tower Road
Beverly Hills, CA 90210
310/276.0666
Fax: 310/276.7291

Ronald Bricke & Associates, Inc.
333 East 69th Street, #7B
New York, NY 10021
212/472.9006
Fax: 212/472.9008
e-mail:rbricke@aol.com

Ruth Livingston Interior Design
74 Main Street
Tiburon, CA 94920
415/435.5361
Fax: 415/435.5361
e-mail: rlstudio@www.ruthlivingston.com

S & B Interiors, Inc.
11270 SW 59th Avenue
Miami, FL 33156
305/661.1572
Fax: 305/661.2722
e-mail: sandb@herald.infi.net

Samuel Botero Associates
420 East 54th Street, Suite 346
New York, NY 10022

Sanford R. Thigpen Interiors, Inc.
2996 Grandview Avenue, Suite 310
Atlanta, GA 30305
404/351.1411
Fax: 404/240.0558

Sara Zook Designs
2001A Youngfield
Golden, CO 80401
303/237.4544
Fax: 303/237.1647

Scott Salvator Inc.
308 East 79th Street
New York, NY 10021
212/861.5355
Fax: 212/861.9557

Sheila Britz Home
1196 Lexington Avenue
New York, NY 10028
212/517.5153
Fax: 212/517.5103

Sistine Interiors
1359 North Beverly Drive
Beverly Hills, CA 90210
310/246.1888
Fax: 310/246.1889
e-mail: boccasi@aol.com

Solis Betancourt
1054 Potomac Street, NW
Washington, DC 20007
202/659.8734
Fax: 202/659.0035

SPACES/Interior Design
4100 Westheimer, #239
Houston, TX.77027
713/622.9696
Fax: 713/622.9699
 e-mail:spaces@internet.mci.com

Stedila Design
135 East 55th Street
New York, NY 10022
212/751.4281
Fax: 212/751.6698

Stingray Hornsby Interior Design
5 The Green
Watertown, CT 06795
860/274.2293
Fax: 860/945.3369
e-mail: stingray@snet.net

Sue Wenk Interior Design
300 East 71st Street
New York, NY 10021
212/879.5149

Susan Fredman & Associates, Ltd.
1510 Old Deerfield Road
Highland Park, IL 60035
847/831.1419
Fax: 847/831.0719

Susan Kroeger, Ltd.
890 Green Bay Road
Winnetka, IL 60093
847/441.0346
Fax: 847/441.0356

Susie Leader Interiors
1280 Latham
Birmingham, MI 48009
248/642.2571
Fax: 248/642.9897
e-mail: suleaderi@aol.com

The Corner Cupboard Antiques and Interiors
615 Tuxedo Place, NW
Atlanta, GA 30342
404/231.9655
Fax: 404/231.5916

Thurston Kitchen and Bath
2920 E 6th Avenue
Denver, CO 80206
303/399.4564
Fax: 303/399.3179

Tomar Lampert Associates
8900 Melrose Avenue, Suite 202
Los Angeles, CA 90069
310/271.4299
Fax: 310/271.1569

Tonin MacCallum ASID Inc.
21 E 90
New York, NY 10128
212/831.8909
Fax: 212/427.2069

Trilogy Village Green
Bedford, NY 10506
914/234.3071
Fax: 914/234.0540

V-3 Design
1212 Avenue of Americas, #802
New York, NY 10036
212/222.2551
Fax: 212/222.2201

VanTosh & Associates
1477 Spring Street
Atlanta, GA 30309
404/888.0613
Fax: 404/876.0191

Vicente Wolf Associates, Inc.
333 West 39th Street
New York, NY 10018
212/465.0590
Fax: 212/465.0639

Visconti and Company
245 E 57th Street
New York, NY 10021

Walker Design Group
7125 E. 2nd Street, #103
Scottsdale, AZ 85251
602/945.1460
Fax: 602/945.1322
e-mail: lwalker@neta.com

William R. Eubanks Interior Design
1516 Union Avenue
Memphis, TN 38104
901/272.1825
Fax: 901/272.1845

∾ *Index* ∾